D1736912

Ambushing

TROPHY WHITETAILS

Tactical Systems for Big-Buck Success

JOHN TROUT, JR.

THE LYONS PRESS
Guilford, Connecticut
An imprint of The Globe Pequot Press

The Lyons Press is an imprint of The Globe Pequot Press.

10 9 8 7 6 5 4 3 2 1

Printed in the United States

ISBN 1-59228-922-3

Library of Congress Cataloging-in-Publication Data is available on file.

To those ethical and creditable deer hunters
who understand the exciting challenge
of honorably pursuing the whitetail
in "Fair Chase" with bow or gun.

Contents

Acknowledgments

This book of ambushing and hunting trophy whitetails did not come easily. It has evolved from numerous years of challenge and dedication. Like any challenging pursuit, the quest has been one of trial and error on my part since I began deer hunting so long ago. Nevertheless, the book's contents are not solely my doing.

First, I would like to thank so many friends, too numerous to mention, who have assisted me in hunting trophy whitetails. My success would not have been possible without their assistance. Oftentimes, their advice was what kept me going. There have been tracking endeavors, hunting adventures, and daily outings in the woods that have become permanent memories, carved into my mind until I take my last breath.

I thank all of my family members for their support, including my four wonderful children, Alisa, Kathy, Tammy and John. I'm grateful to John, with whom I have shared many rewarding and unforgettable experiences, for our hunting companionship. We live many miles apart, but our frequent phone discussions of "bucks" heartily fulfill my off-hours.

I owe special thanks to my wife Vikki, and to my dad who recently passed his 81st birthday. Dad is the one who showed me the ropes, so to speak, more than 40 years ago. He still manages to spend a few hours in the woods each year, and I'm so glad he does. And I owe thanks to Vikki for being a sincere hunting buddy who makes each trip to the woods more pleasurable, even when

I see nothing from my stand. I also appreciate her assistance in proofreading the pages that follow. She has spent countless hours in front of the computer.

Every aspiring hunting writer hopes his beliefs and tactics can be read by others. This book might not have been possible without the people at The Lyons Press, who undertook the job of editing and publishing my work. I also thank the many magazine editors who have done the same over the years.

I appreciate the Pope and Young Club and Boone and Crockett Club for allowing me to use statistics within this book. Additionally, I admire both clubs for their continued advocacy of fair-chase hunting, which provides reassurance that tomorrow's hunters can enjoy the same challenges we have.

I thank F+W Publications, publishers of *Deer & Deer Hunting* magazine for allowing me to use statistics. I also thank their editors, and particularly Dan Schmidt, for the encouragement and writing opportunities he has provided to me over the years.

In the final chapter of this book, a few great whitetail hunters speak out. I thank Jim Hole, Jr., Tim Hilsmeyer, Jeff Hintz, Peter Fiduccia, Gabe Shaffner, Jay Cassell, and Eddie Salter for sharing their astounding knowledge. I have learned much from them, and I hope that you will also.

Lastly, I thank the Lord for his wonderful creations, from the hardwoods to the mountains, and for my health that enables me to continue enjoying the serenity of the beautiful and fascinating outdoors.

Introduction

The pursuit of trophy whitetails has drastically intensified in recent years. Before deer populations exploded, and when many states and provinces were more interested in increasing rather than decreasing herd numbers, many hunters were happy with tagging any antlerless deer or yearling buck, and rightfully so. There is still nothing wrong with shooting and tagging any legal deer, and it is a necessary management tool.

Consider 1958, when my dad shot his first buck with bow and arrow while hunting southern Indiana. The hunting seasons were short, and few deer were harvested. Like all hunters back then, he would have been happy to shoot a young buck (antlerless deer were not allowed). However, a two-year-old eight-pointer happened to pass his ground blind. The buck made the newspapers, and folks came from miles away to see the buck hanging in our garage.

Although many of us now pursue record-book bucks aggressively, hunters must continue to control deer herds. We have to shoot does, and we have to provide enough opportunity for hunters to get the job done. Hunting is the most effective method of herd reduction.

On the other hand, who can deny the super challenge of ambushing a monster buck? Most dedicated trophy hunters have been around for a while. They have harvested several deer, and they do not find a challenge in shooting just any deer. As the consequences have accumulated over recent decades, we can partly blame increasing deer herds and hunting opportunities on the increasing number of trophy hunters. Hunters who once found satisfaction in shooting a deer now find satisfaction only in shooting a wall-hanger.

In short, that is the primary reason for this book. And while the pursuit of huge bucks has become popular, so have the tactics with which we pursue them. These tactics continue to develop; we have only recently perfected the ambush that has led to the demise of many wall-hangers. You could rely on Lady Luck, and while it's true that she is responsible for many dead bucks each season, it requires determination, knowledge of a big buck's habits, and advanced strategies to achieve close-range shooting opportunities.

I would like to emphasize the "close-range" topic. The central point of this book is to increase your chance of having a close-range encounter with a huge buck. The majority of big bucks I have shot were very close when they were ambushed, and there's a good reason for this. I'm both a bowhunter and gun hunter. I have never considered myself a top-notch shooter with bow and arrow. In fact, my effective shooting range has always been, and I suspect always will be, 25 yards or less. As for the firearm seasons, most of my hunting has been with a muzzleloader and slugster. My slug gun is the old traditional smoothbore, with an effective shooting range of 60 yards. These limits have, however, made me a better hunter. I know that I must have a close encounter to be successful, and that ambush strategies must be perfected if I am to have a close encounter with a mature whitetail buck. I also know that the closer he is, the better the chance he will fall.

After mentioning "ambush tactics" in previous paragraphs, and throughout the rest of the book for that matter, you should know that this includes an array of tried-and-true situations. There is no sure-fire tactic for ambushing a mature whitetail buck. Some tactics are seasonal. Some tactics apply only when the breeding begins. Some tactics are dependent upon food sources. Some tactics relate to hunting pressure, weather, buck sign, bedding areas, etc. You see, it's not a matter of just knowing when a buck is vulnerable. It's a matter of knowing the proverbial "who, what, when, and where" that makes him vulnerable. While it might only take one ambush tactic to put a big one down, it could involve several methods. Many times, ambushing the right buck is like assembling a puzzle.

Unfortunately, the new era of trophy hunting has led to canned hunts and illegal hunting practices. Although North America's primary record clubs (Boone and Crockett, and Pope and Young) clearly state that animals must be harvested in "fair chase," this has not had an effect on some individuals. In fact, many canned hunts now exist solely for the antlers. In case you didn't know, canned hunts are those that occur behind a high fence. We shouldn't, however, call this hunting. None of the trophy photos you will see in this book came from an enclosure; they were all taken in fair chase.

In the pages that follow, you'll gain valuable insights for ambushing mature and educated bucks with both bow and gun. I have hunted for more than four decades with a large emphasis on bowhunting, and have found that bowhunting strategies have helped me to enjoy more success with a firearm. Although this book provides advanced tactics, it is laid out in an easy-to-follow manner to help any hunter who hopes to put a buck on the wall consistently with bow or gun.

You won't find chapters related to just bowhunting strategies, or just gun-hunting methods. They are combined throughout the book, and you will read about particular weapons as they apply in specific anecdotes and strategies. You are already aware that season dates vary from one area to another, and that most areas offer more archery days than gun-hunting opportunities. Primary rut dates also vary from region to region, and this affects both the archery and firearm enthusiast. The tactics mentioned in the pages that follow apply to all.

This would be a good time to clarify the differences between ambushing old bucks and young bucks. Big bucks don't make mistakes as often as little bucks. They require more patterning, and they are much better at making sure they are one step ahead of you. This book will help you to overcome their wariness and stay one step ahead of them.

This volume will not provide shooting tips. Nor will it provide locations of lodges and names of outfitters that provide you with assurance of killing a whopper buck. It is a book for the hunter who loves the challenge of pursuing a buck with big antlers, one-on-one. Whether you hunt close to home, or travel to other states for a week-long pursuit, it provides the information and strategies you need for an opportunity to kill a super buck.

The book is divided into two sections. Section I provides tactical issues essential for pursuing and ambushing mature bucks successfully, from food sources to knowing a big one when you see one. Section II analyzes specialized tactics you can't afford to overlook. A few chapters provide tales of big bucks and how they met their demise, clearly demonstrating the effects of specialized ambush tactics.

I also urge you to pay close attention to how Section I portrays the entire rut cycle. Most deaths of whopper bucks are related in one way or another to breeding. Chapter 2 covers a lot of ground, from the earliest stage of pre-rut to the second and final rut. Lady Luck may heartily contribute during the peak of the rut, more often than the best of hunters in fact, but this chapter will help you ambush a super buck without relying on that buck to make a mistake.

Although I've taken several mature bucks, I don't claim to know everything about big bucks. Each season I do either of two things: tag one or more whopper bucks, or commit an error that cost me one or more whopper bucks. The commonality between the two rests upon opportunities. I always have one or more opportunities to kill a big buck before the hunting seasons end. Unfortunately, over the years the opportunities I've messed up have exceeded the number of bucks I've harvested. The truth is, I think more often about those that got away than those hanging on the wall. After all, we learn far more from mistakes than achievements, which is why you should carefully read Chapter 18 in Section II, "Ambush Errors." Following that is another important chapter that describes how easily big bucks make errors, even if you do everything wrong.

I've included tips from many veteran whitetail hunters, all of whom consistently take super bucks. Some names you may recognize, and some you may not. Although these guys know their stuff, they are folks just like you, who love to hunt and love the challenge of pursuing a huge buck. Some are primarily archery hunters; some hunt primarily with guns. A couple of these hunters include still-hunting methods. Many hunters might not think of still-hunting as an ambush method, but in all reality, it is. Their comments and tips are sure to help your chances of tagging a big buck.

I will be the first to admit: regardless of the strategies I've learned, and those that I thought I knew, there's always more to the story. In fact, I learn something new each season. Many veteran deer hunters who have taken their share of big bucks will openly say the same. We've learned a lot about ambushing trophy bucks, but the need to learn more continues. If you feel the same way, you'll want to read on.

SECTION I

CHAPTER 1

Big Bucks, Big Bellies:
Creating the Food Ambush

Methodology for ambushing a deer near a food source is nothing new. Magazine articles continue to discuss details of such strategies, talking about the proverbial "setting up on trails between the food source and the bedding area." When it comes to surprising a big buck near a food source, however, I suggest you forget about the proverbial strategies and setups.

First, I want to clarify that big bucks do not differ from other deer when it comes to food choices. They eat the same foods as do subordinate bucks, does, and fawns. But that's the only similarity. When it comes to feeding habits—when and where he feeds in daylight hours—a mature buck differs from other deer.

Several weeks or even months before the rut, a buck is compelled to eat hardy. This is necessary in view of what lies ahead, and he is instinctively aware of the proper nutrients needed for the body fat that will keep him moving consistently in search of breeding does. Bucks do feed during the rut, but it doesn't compare to time spent doing so before and after. He will gladly pass up a meal to spend time with the ladies. After the exertion of the

Food is an essential factor for determining proper
stand placement in most cases.

rut, he must again depend upon plentiful nutrition to get him
through the winter.

With that said, you might have the idea that all you must do is
find a food source to ambush the buck of your dreams, and there is
some truth to that statement. A food source could provide the perfect ambush location at any phase of the rut and put a monster buck
within easy bow or gun range. But food sources can change rapidly
without warning. You might waste time at the wrong one, or spend
time at a food source that a buck avoids during daylight hours.

Understanding the Food Sources

Before getting into specific food sources and hot ambush locations, be aware that there are two primary types of foods a big buck might visit consistently: isolated foods and fields. The former include mast supplied by Mother Nature, and are typically located in dense areas. Fields are sometimes provided by Mother Nature, but most often are agricultural in origin and located in open areas.

Deer also feed on a variety of woody and non-woody plants, but these seldom provide ambush possibilities until the secluded mast sources and fields no longer provide sustenance. This is often the case in winter.

Whitetails prefer foods that provide the most nutrition. When these foods are not available, they resort to what is. Some areas offer more preferred foods than others do, but it is vitally important for you to know which foods provide the best opportunity to ambush a trophy whitetail.

Specific nutrition sources can often be the key in zeroing in on a big buck's feeding habits.

Finally, you must know how hunting pressure could affect a food source and ambush location. Big bucks are survival specialists. They won't tolerate consistent—or even inconsistent—intrusion, and they will abandon food sources if necessary. Here's a look at foods that provide ambush possibilities, and how you should go about the ambush.

The Oak Phenomenon

Many big bucks fall only because hunters locate isolated acorns. I've taken super whitetails during all phases of the rut, and only because I found hot oaks in the right area when acorns were available.

Sometimes a mature buck will visit the acorns to feed. But don't think for a moment that big bucks make consistent trips to the oak merely to feed on acorns. During the pre-rut period, many bucks will visit secluded oaks to stuff their gut, but as the rut nears, they often make stopovers to see who has been there. After all, they know the oak is also attracting does and is therefore a likely spot to pick up the hot trail of a doe nearing estrus.

Oaks are somewhat cyclic. Some produce acorns one year and not the next. Some always seem to produce when conditions are favorable. Weather has a significant effect on this, which means good years and bad years. When a healthy mast occurs, it's common for deer to head for the oaks, passing up delightful crops and other natural foods to get to the acorns. Acorns are not only tasty to deer, but also high in protein.

Spring weather often determines acorn production. An unexpected, hard spring freeze will often play havoc with buds and could keep oaks from producing. Location of the oak is often a factor, since cold temperatures typically affect many oaks in low-lying areas. It's also true that a severe summer drought can impair mast production.

The point is, you can't necessarily count on the same oak to provide opportunity year after year. Some years you can count on finding numerous acorns. Some years you will find a limited number of acorns, or perhaps even none.

Limited mast is the best scenario for the trophy hunter. When several oaks produce mast, deer do not need to move as far to locate the acorns. Less movement means less chance of ambushing a passing buck. It's also true that you cannot pattern a buck as effectively when there is an abundance of acorns, because the bucks have more places to go and do not have to visit the oak where you set up your ambush. When the supply is limited, though, you can pinpoint with accuracy where the deer will be.

There are two primary families of oaks: red and white, and there are several types of oak in each. Acorns of each species provide nutrition, and deer will feed on any or all. However, some taste better and are preferred by deer more than others. We also know that the acorns of some oaks attract deer before others do. For these reasons, you should have an understanding of the oaks in your region, and be able to identify each species.

A trained eye can often determine the type of oak by the bark of the tree, but a glance at the leaves provides no doubt as to the family of oak to which the tree belongs. For example, the lobes of red oak leaves are pointed, whereas the lobes of white oak leaves are rounded. Sizes and shapes of leaves vary from one species to another, but the leaves' lobes provide a quick and accurate identification. A few species of oak leaves do not have individual lobes and are oval instead. I won't get into the numerous varieties of oaks, but will say that red and white oaks are the most abundant and grow heartily in many regions.

White oak acorns taste sweeter than those of the red oak family, and this undoubtedly plays a role in a deer's preference. Deer will often pass up red oak acorns to get to a white oak that is shedding acorns consistently. This rule is not carved in stone, since some white oaks might produce very little mast some seasons while red oaks produce great quantities.

Because germination begins later in red oaks, white oak acorns typically ripen before acorns of the red oaks. Once the acorns start falling, they are usually ready for consumption. Many white oaks begin dropping acorns in early autumn and attract deer immediately. Red oaks usually begin shedding their acorns a few weeks later. Once the white oak acorns stop falling, red oak acorns become the favorite. Again, though, there are no set rules governing this transition. Weather and location will influence oaks and their germination behavior.

No oak sheds acorns throughout the hunting season. I have seen some oaks shed acorns and attract deer for only a few days, and I have seen others attract deer for weeks. It depends upon the abundance of mast, but all oaks have a limit. When the food source is plentiful, the bucks will be there. As the food dwindles, so will the deer.

Rain, wind, and frost are often responsible for acorn falls. All oaks will shed their acorns in due time, but weather could prompt the process. In fact, rain and/or wind one day could make the hunting great the following day.

I don't believe that any other food source is capable of attracting mature bucks as often as acorns. Although oaks are like other foods in that they are seasonal, they are capable of lasting longer. I've had action in early fall, late fall, and even early winter. As long as you can locate acorns, deer may well come.

Just because you locate an oak that sheds acorns, it doesn't necessarily mean that you have found an oak that will attracts a big buck, or other deer for that matter. Sign will be plentiful if deer visit the oak regularly. Droppings are usually abundant and found within the immediate vicinity of the tree. Leaves on the woods floor will also appear distorted as deer scoot them to the sides to locate the fallen acorns. These areas appear a little like turkey scratchings, but somewhat smaller. Deer seldom paw the ground, however, as some hunters believe. They actually use their noses to locate the acorns, moving the leaves in the process.

You can often hear the sounds of deer feeding on acorns. A "popping" noise occurs as deer crack the acorns and the caps that cover them. When studying captive whitetails, I often observed deer feeding on acorns. Some deer did not mind eating both the cap and acorn, while others preferred to let the cap fall and eat only the acorn.

Secluded oaks usually provide the best results and are more likely to attract a mature buck in daylight hours. Seldom will I set up an ambush site by oaks along the fringes—unless hunting pressure is minimal, and it's nearly impossible to reach other hot oaks without bumping into the wall-hanger I hope to kill. I firmly

believe that the denser the area, the better the chance an educated and mature buck will show.

Once you have located a hot oak, you have two choices: You
can either set up along the trails leading to and from the oak, or
you can set up at the oak. There are pros and cons to both, but I
often prefer the "closer is better" method.

Although there are many differences between hunting for a
buck near an oak and hunting over bear bait, there are similarities. For instance, in both cases you can assume that the food
source is where the animal will inevitably wind up (assuming wind
direction doesn't cause trouble). The trail leading to and from
might not be the route the animal uses. I therefore prefer setting
up within a few yards of the oak, and occasionally in the oak itself.
The gunner doesn't have to be as meticulous, but bowhunters will
experience more positive results if they stay as close to the
acorns as possible. I have always opted for the latter approach,
regardless of whether I hunt with bow or gun.

I won't go into the importance of wind direction and how it
can hurt an ambush site. You already know this. But it is worth
keeping in mind that it is far easier to have favorable wind when
you set up at the oak. If you plan the ambush away from the food
source, it's much more difficult to play the wind. Big bucks don't
always travel with the wind in their nose, but they seldom travel
with the wind at their rump. Many will travel through a crosswind.
In other words, wind direction may come from their left or right.
Thus, I would suggest you set up on the acorns where the wind is
blowing in the direction you least expect the buck to come from,
or where a crosswind will exist. You can sometimes beat a crosswind, but you won't beat a buck that has his nose into the wind.

As the rut progresses, they will visit the oaks to locate does. During each phase, they will often leave behind valuable, telltale buck sign for all to see. This is one indication of who has visited the acorns, and a mature buck that comes once will probably come again. (Later chapters discuss deciphering buck sign and ambushing the buck responsible.)

Other Isolated Foods

Acorns are perhaps the hottest secluded foods available to the whitetail, but they are not the only ones that provide excellent ambush opportunities for big bucks. In the right location, any of a number of secluded foods will bring the right buck in, sometimes long after dawn or long before dark.

You can find other secluded foods in nearly every geographical location, but like acorns, they are seasonal. For instance, domestic apples and crabapples, as well as several other fruits, can be productive. Persimmons are also plentiful throughout much of North America, and have produced action for many hunters.

Several years ago, I located a crabapple tree right in the middle of a dense stand of saplings during the early archery season, long before the peak rut. Both the tree and the ground were laced with the sour apples. I had not seen a mature buck in the area, but nearby rubs indicated one had been there. Although I had to set up some 40 yards from the thicket, it paid off the first evening I hunted. One hour before dusk, an eight-pointer appeared. He came in to the apple tree out of bow range, but fifteen minutes later walked past me. My arrow zipped through the buck as he stood only a few yards from my tree stand.

Several factors contributed to patterning that buck. This isolated food allowed any deer to visit and feel secure. Deer droppings were abundant near the crabapple tree. Food was still available on the ground and above, which indicated deer would return. The huge rubs provided a positive ID that the right buck had been there and would likely return.

Persimmons have also provided me with plenty of action. Deer prefer them most after the first frost. Availability and location often determine how effectively they attract deer, however. Although some persimmon trees in heavily wooded areas don't produce as much fruit as those along fringes and in thickets where the sun can reach them, I have patterned bucks in almost every location where persimmons were available.

Persimmons are usually most attractive to deer after the first frost, and after hunting pressure accelerates.

Many berries also allow patterning opportunities, providing they produce a great amount of soft mast. However, as cold weather prevails and natural mast and agricultural foods fade, it could come down to finding natural green foliage such as honeysuckle. Honeysuckle flourishes in many areas and provides thick cover that big bucks dearly love. It is strong and hardy, and offers succulent green leaves even after the first few freezes.

If snow falls and covers other foods, honeysuckle will attract deer immediately and consistently. Consider my late-season firearm hunt two years ago. Two inches of snow fell, but I stuck with my ambush location near a wheat field. After failing to see a buck the first couple of evenings, I headed for a secluded and dense honeysuckle thicket to set up a new stand. The area was riddled with big buck sign. On the first evening, a respectable nine-pointer came walking in only an hour after I arrived on stand. My slugster roared as the buck passed within 40 yards of the stand.

This example is not intended to show that honeysuckle becomes hot only after snow. On the contrary, honeysuckle is an isolated food that provides action as soon as other food sources dry up, or when hunting pressure pushes deer and big bucks away from fields. Snow might make it easier to pattern a buck near honeysuckle, but honeysuckle could attract a buck anytime.

I would also suggest you consider searching for honey locust trees. Their produce is often plentiful, and often found in secluded locations. Honey locusts are a member of the bean family and produce a large pod (sometimes six to eight inches long) containing the seeds. Most deer pay little attention to the pods until they have been on the ground for a while, but they can become hot overnight. Just last year, my wife Vikki and I each hunted a stand near a honey locust tree. We saw numerous deer over a three-week period, including one super buck that failed to walk into bow range.

One of the keys to hunting isolated foods is being able to recognize them. If not familiar with these natural food sources, I suggest you take a crash course before attempting to pattern a buck. Many books are available that provide photos and/or illustrations of plants and trees, mast or fruit they produce, and regional areas where they are found. Here are a couple that can help: *Trees of North America* by C. Frank Robinson, published by Golden Press, provides numerous color illustrations of major trees and mast, as well as range maps. Western and Eastern editions of *Familiar Trees of North America* from the National Audubon Society are pocket-sized books that you can carry with you in the field. Published by Alfred A. Knopf, they include color illustrations and concise identification methods.

You can also learn much on your own by searching for secluded foods and exercising patience while carefully examining the area. Numerous fresh droppings near the food source provide proof that deer come consistently. You can assume that a mature buck is likely to visit the same secluded foods as do antlerless deer, but clear buck sign nearby is definitely a plus. Always keep a close eye on the food source you hunt and make certain you change ambush locations as soon as the mast diminishes, or when sightings stop. Once you hunt a food source a few times, it could dry up quickly even if mast remains.

Getting to and from Isolated Foods

Trophy hunters have to be concerned with locating isolated foods, setting up the ambush, and then hunting the big buck that uses the area. More than once in this book, you will read and understand how mature bucks are seldom forgiving. We might as well start here: Make one mistake, and it could be over.

When scouting farmlands, many trophy hunters can locate bucks while staying in their vehicles, and without penetrating the area. This is not possible when you attempt to find isolated foods and big bucks that use them. Unfortunately, any time you penetrate dense areas, you run the risk of a whopper buck detecting your presence. Moreover, you must also penetrate the area each time you hunt a big buck near an isolated food source. It's tricky business, and vital that you never assume that you will avoid detection.

I can't tell you how nervous I become when walking close to or into an area that could hide a super whitetail. Think how easily your hunt could end if he knows you are there. Worse, it can happen without you knowing, in which case you could spend time hunting an isolated food source that a big buck has deserted.

Always avoid coming into contact with brush and debris that could retain your scent. Does and insubordinate bucks will tolerate much more disturbance than educated whitetails will. Select locations with sparser vegetation in which to walk, and always avoid penetrating thickets where big bucks could be bedded.

I also suggest you do your moving at opportune times. Don't scout for isolated foods when big bucks are likely to be moving. Midday offers the best opportunities. Even scouting during late morning and early afternoon can be risky. After a big buck becomes accustomed to visiting a favorite isolated food, and has been left undisturbed, he won't necessarily restrict his movements to only dusk and dawn.

Always set up tree stands as quietly as possible. The same goes for clearing shooting lanes. It's far better to sacrifice shooting opportunities on a huge buck that may arrive than to have plenty of shots at a buck that never shows up.

When hunting the non-acorn isolated food sources, you should follow the same tactics mentioned for hunting oaks. Set up as close to the food as possible. Also, consider that you are on borrowed time once the hunting starts. In fact, it's only a matter of time until a big buck knows you are there, or have been there. It's virtually impossible to hunt a food source consistently and remain undetected. One should therefore assume that the best chance of ambushing that buck will occur the first few times you hunt. If it doesn't happen then, odds are you will need to move on to another ambushing possibility.

Agri-Handouts

There was a day when I relied almost totally on secluded foods for patterning a buck utilizing a food source, but today I rely equally on agri-foods simply because the area I hunt is not as pressured.

With suburbanization occurring rapidly, it's no wonder that many deer hunters depend greatly upon agricultural areas to harvest a deer. Nonetheless, timing is often just as vital a part of ambushing a super buck near these food sources. You might pattern the right buck, only to have him be elsewhere while you wait for him to appear along the best agricultural food source of the area.

Before going on, let me first clarify how hunting pressure greatly affects how often a buck visits an agricultural food source. Light to moderate pressure probably won't keep the old-timers away, but too much activity will make sure a buck won't be in the open arena except when darkness prevails.

Several years ago, while hunting Alberta's Bow Zone, I couldn't believe how many big bucks would arrive in open fields in daylight hours. Granted, it was usually late evening, but their habits were nevertheless far different than in areas I hunted in the U.S. Midwest where hunting pressure made certain the experienced bucks stayed clear of the open fields. For this reason, always consider hunting pressure when deciding whether to hunt agricultural fields or isolated foods. Isolated foods often allow morning and evening opportunities, whereas agricultural foods primarily provide evening ambush opportunities. Also, consider that in some areas you can start the season trying to ambush a super buck near a field, and then resort to penetrating the area's internal regions to find other foods after the pressure accelerates.

I'm sure you are already aware of the hottest agricultural foods in your area. Hunters probably rely on corn and soybeans most often to pattern a super buck. These seasonal food sources vary considerably in nutrition, with corn providing far less protein than soybeans. Let's look at some considerations of ambushing super bucks at agricultural foods.

Deer don't actually feed on the soybean pods. They begin browsing the leaves early in summer shortly after the plants are out of the ground. Big bucks seldom visit soybean fields in autumn, unless it was a late-planted field that continues to provide green leaves. Many hunters waste time in ambush near soybean fields where they might see a big buck in late summer. Most mature whitetails abandon these fields by the time the first hunting season arrives, although they may still attract does and fawns. It is prudent, however, to keep an eye on soybean fields that are harvested early. Favorable warm weather often prompts new green sprouts to develop during hunting seasons. I've seen the new sprouts attract a big buck for a second time after believing the field was dead.

Cornfields can attract mature bucks before harvesting. They provide a bedding area with security at its finest, and food as the corn nears harvest time. Additionally, as corn stalks mature, they provide shade and temperatures that are cooler than in other bedding areas.

Locating a trophy buck might be difficult, but if you know that a certain buck visits the standing corn, an opportunity exists to make a successful ambush. During late summer, just two weeks before preparing this chapter, I spotted three bucks leave a standing cornfield at dusk. One could assume that all three bucks had been bedded in the field throughout the day. The last of the bunch sported a healthy pair of antlers and offered promise for a future ambush.

Ambushing a buck near standing corn has its challenges, and the primary aisles bordering the field usually offer the best opportunity. It's a matter of locating the best sign along the fringes, and setting up within shooting range of the aisle. Look for numerous and large tracks, or perhaps early-season rubs against the timber bordering the aisle.

Once corn is harvested, the field is right for hunting. It doesn't take long for most deer to come to the field consistently. Within twenty-four hours of harvest, you can bet the field will provide an ambush opportunity—if a big buck is in the area and hunting pressure does not intensify.

Some harvested cornfields are cleaner than others. The more kernels of corn that remain, the better the chance deer—including a big buck—will visit the field. Nevertheless, you might have

Both standing corn and harvested cornfields offer opportunities, but it's important to time the food source accurately.

only a short window of time to get the job done. A harvested corn-field could become active within twenty-four hours, but will prob-ably offer the best ambushing opportunity for only the first few days following harvest. Then the action tapers. Some cornfields will continue to attract whitetails many weeks or even months after the harvest, but the super bucks will often avoid the fields in daylight hours shortly after harvesting. With this in mind, you can assume that the better ambush locations might be away from the field a week to ten days following harvest.

Alfalfa and clover are the hottest green fields before cold tem-peratures prevail, and are capable of attracting big bucks consis-tently if hunting pressure remains minimal. The green fields also are more reliable for a longer period than cornfields and soy-beans. However, even their days are numbered. After a few hard freezes, the plants stop growing and wither. Although these fields are occasionally cut for hay during summer and early autumn, they provide excellent possibilities for patterning a buck up until the thermometer crashes.

Winter wheat, on the other hand, usually attracts deer best when other agricultural handouts are no longer available. While bowhunting last December, a few weeks after the peak rut, I missed my shot at a super buck near dusk, just 25 yards before it would have stepped into a winter wheat field. Winter wheat does not grow much during the winter, but if it develops readily in autumn, it will produce action in the cold weather as other food sources dwindle.

Oats, millet, milo, and other agri-foods provide opportunity for an ambush, but the possibility of a successful ambush de-pends upon your timing and your setup. There's never a guaran-tee where a buck will appear. Although the gunner has an extended range, the bowhunter must hope the buck will come to the field within close proximity. Always use logical analysis when choosing the best ambush location. Again, setting up close to the food source is usually the best option.

Avoid setting up in a line of trees in the middle of a field, unless wind direction forces you to stay away from the fringes of the cover and field. The best opportunities often lie along sides of hills where you find the thickest cover bordering the field. In flat areas, you also will have the best chance of ambushing a mature whitetail near the thickest fringes. There may be exceptions, due to terrain and location of the dense cover, but most often a mature buck will select a vantage point in which he can remain hidden to view the field.

Once deer activity slows, or if you fail to see the right buck, it's probably time to make a move. You could consider penetrating the area and selecting a new ambush location a short distance from the field, which will increase your chance of seeing a super buck during daylight hours.

Scouting and getting to agri-foods is seldom a problem like isolated foods. Farmland hunters can usually walk the open areas and create little or no disturbance. However, one problem exists after setting up and attempting to ambush a big buck near an agricultural food source. Other deer are often nearby when it comes time to leave in the evenings, and they can act as sentries. For this reason, I would suggest you stay on stand as late as possible. I can't tell you how many times I've stayed put long after dark. Spooking does and insubordinate bucks might not appear as bad as sending the big one into the next county, but the results could be the same. Many big bucks get close to open fields but avoid walking into them until darkness prevails. If they are close by, other deer will send up the red flag that could spoil your hunt the next evening. The darker it is when you leave, the better.

Perhaps the best take-home message for hunting food sources is to remember that they offer opportunities for a brief time. Seldom does a food provide opportunity throughout a hunting season. You must be there when it's hot, but move onto other possibilities if they fail. Typically, the hot period for big bucks is brief. You can wager that a mature buck will know you are there, or have been there, if you hunt food sources consistently.

CHAPTER 2

The Rut: *Before, During, and After*

I n breeding matters, there are two tactical issues to be broken down: how and when bucks are moving during each phase of the rut, and how patterning does can lead you to a mature buck.

The breeding cycle is responsible for the death of most trophy whitetails. They start making mistakes just before the breeding

Once the breeding begins, bucks will come out of the woodwork. Movement will intensify for days to come after the rut peaks, providing hunting pressure remains minimal.

cycle begins, and they don't stop until it ends. Don't think for a moment that the breeding cycle refers to only the primary rut—on the contrary, the breeding cycle lasts for months, from early autumn through the post-rut.

Understanding the myths and facts surrounding each phase of the rut is necessary for those who pursue mature whitetail bucks. The habits of a buck change during each phase of the rut, and so must ambushing tactics. For instance, hunting trails, food sources, bedding areas, rubs, scrapes, and more can be used at some point during the breeding cycle to ambush a super whitetail. But there isn't any one tactical approach that applies to each phase of the rut. Some are better in pre-rut, while others might work best when bucks pursue does.

Reluctant Pre-Rut Movements

The long days of summer and sunlight have dwindled, and photoperiodism is about to become the factor that will affect bucks for months to come. Photoperiodism is the decrease in sunlight that causes a buck's testicles to enlarge and his testosterone to rise. This is known as the pre-rut phase—the first segment of the rut when all bucks begin rubbing antlers and sparring. At this time, mature bucks are creatures of habit, sticking to smaller ranges and traveling common routes.

Contrary to many hunters' beliefs, the pre-rut period can offer excellent opportunities to ambush a mature buck. He is reluctant to move long distances in search of does, but because his movements are limited, the best opportunity exists to pattern a super whitetail. I discuss the home-range factors and patterning tactics, which are vital for ambushing a buck during the pre-rut, in Chapter 3.

A buck's range begins to expand late in the pre-rut when he begins to pursue does. Young bucks begin earlier during the pre-rut phase, as they "bird dog" both mature does and doe fawns. The big boys don't have a problem with the one-and-a-half-year-old bucks making fools of themselves. They know the breeding won't begin for a while, and they save their strength for better times to come.

The entire length of the pre-rut period can vary geographically, but a safe assumption is about eight to ten weeks. In other words, about sixty days will elapse from the shedding of the velvet to the primary breeding cycle. And while photoperiodism affects bucks, it also works on the mature does. You won't notice it until the breeding begins; it's like a silent phase of the rut. On the other hand, the bucks are well aware when a doe's urge to breed nears. While remaining somewhat dormant, the mature bucks follow the does' patterns closely, keeping an alert watch for the right day.

How Bucks Move During the Rut

The peak rut period is limited to a period of about two weeks, although hunting pressure might reduce that time span. For about fourteen days, mature bucks turn it on and often move consistently in search of does. During this period there is a "peak day" when the breeding jumps into high gear. This is the day that many mature does breed, and when bucks, including the big ones that have not yet been active, could move at any hour of the day.

The peak day can often be determined with a great deal of accuracy by veteran hunters. That's not to say they pick the exact day, but they are able to determine that it will occur within a span of a few days. The peak of the breeding period varies from one area to another, but it typically falls about the same time in the same area each year. Latitude determines when the breeding begins. In the Midwest where I reside, I can count on the peak day to occur between November 12 and 16. In many areas of the South, the peak day could fall in late December or sometime in January.

Large antlers make a difference in deciding who does the breeding. Unquestionably, big racks intimidate young bucks. However, body size and physical condition also play important roles, particularly when two mature bucks pursue an estrous doe.

The bucks know both when a doe is about to breed and that does move more during the breeding cycle. According to a 1975 study conducted by J. J. Ozoga and L. J. Verme, a doe's nighttime activity increases sharply when her estrogen production surges, just before mating begins. She frequently urinates and expels pheromones, which bucks detect easily. Biologists have shown that a doe is in heat for about twenty-four hours. Breeding occurs during this short time, and the peak-rut day becomes history.

Not surprisingly, many states and provinces time the firearm season for the arrival of the primary rut. Harvests are higher at this time of the season, and all bucks, big and small, do stupid things. What is surprising, though, is the number of hunters that choose only to hunt during the primary rut. I don't agree that you should wait for the peak-rut period to attempt to ambush a mature buck, but I do know that the way to get the job done is to pattern the does.

Patterning Does

One of the biggest mistakes a trophy hunter can make is patterning the does when it doesn't count. For instance, many early-season archery hunters plan their ambush location around the hottest trails and foods where they've found the most deer sign. Firearm hunters who have the opportunity to hunt before and after the rut follow suit. If the hunter finds numerous tracks and droppings, the location becomes irresistible.

I won't deny the benefits of locating abundant deer sign. It certainly increases your chance of ambushing a doe, fawn, or possibly an insubordinate buck any time during the hunting season. However, if the breeding is yet to come, or has passed, your chance of intercepting a super buck drastically diminishes. Before the rut, many of the big ones simply haven't come out of the woodwork yet.

During the peak rut, when the breeding is either imminent or underway, there is a window of opportunity to pattern the does and kill the buck of your dreams. Remember that mature bucks know when the breeding will begin. It's not a guessing game, and they seldom waste their time in hot doe areas until then—super bucks don't seek and respond to does until it counts. But once the big boys know the time is right, they will be where the does are, albeit briefly.

Lip curling is one form of behavior exhibited by bucks during the rut. The lip is pulled back, which closes the nasal chamber and intensifies the doe's odor, helping him to determine the stage of estrus.

Hot and Cold Trails

During the pre-rut, mature and educated bucks often travel the secondary trails—the ones that many hunters walk right past and don't notice. These secondary trails are not where the hunter should be once the breeding begins, however. In fact, these trails become cold almost overnight.

Once the breeding is about to begin, primary trails attract the huge bucks. Primary trails show up readily because they have been there for eons and are carved into the landscape. But avoid the mistake of setting up on a primary trail that is not attracting does. Sign and particularly abundant droppings indicate an active primary trail.

The primary trails that attract does are those that lead them to the basics: food and bedding grounds. That might sound more like a trail to ambush a little buck, but during the peak rut, mature bucks will follow the same trails as the young bucks and does. This is exactly how many big bucks make their last mistake. When the breeding begins, they must travel the hottest trails to find does. That's not to say, though, that any well-used trail provides a great opportunity for ambushing a big buck. Mature bucks particularly like specific primary travel routes, especially those that allow them to intercept other trails in the least amount of time.

Big Bucks and Natural Travel Corridors

Although fencelines, funnels, and other travel corridors can provide usable trails throughout the fall and winter months, these areas are that much more attractive to big bucks during the rut. First, consider diminishing foliage. In early autumn, many areas contain foliage. By the time the rut arrives, much of the foliage has dissipated. Travel corridors provide cover and rate far above the common trails of the open hardwoods.

Even better, though, is what a mature buck stands to gain when traveling natural travel corridors, or funnels (pockets of thickets or timber within open areas). Whether it's a fenceline, a wooded narrow draw, or perhaps a ditchline, a big buck knows he will cross several other trails that could allow him to intercept a doe. When the breeding begins, mature bucks don't waste time. They want to cover ground and follow routes that cross with other trails. That's exactly what travel corridors do.

A few years ago, I set up along a thick fenceline, bordered by hardwoods on one side and open slots and thickets on the other. A trail followed the fenceline for several hundred yards, and a few additional trails crossed the fenceline trail. The first evening, an eight-pointer walked the fenceline with his nose to the ground. He was intent on picking up the trail of a doe near one of the fence openings. In fact, he might have done so had my slugster not ended his enterprise.

Fence crossings are fantastic locations to set up during the breeding period, providing a trail exists. You can bet that every big buck knows where these crossings are, and is likely to consistently travel the fences to locate them in hopes of picking up a doe.

Funnels and bottlenecks are also attractive because super bucks know the does are using them by the time the rut arrives, and they know that there will be several other trails they can intercept, just like the buck that followed the fenceline. These travel routes often provide the best cover and, if they connect to other favorable areas, will become consistent whitetail highways.

However, the key to funnels' and bottlenecks' potential is what lies on each end. If they connect to foods and/or timber and thickets, they have what it takes to attract the does and big bucks. In many agricultural areas, such funnels and bottlenecks can be positively the best for ambushing a mature buck during the rut, primarily because of limited travel routes in open country.

The more vast timber that exists, the more difficult it becomes to locate and effectively hunt a funnel or bottleneck.

When setting up in these travel corridors, use common sense and select a location where you can cover it best. The wider the corridor, the more difficult it is to cover. If the corridor leads to a food source, such as crops, stick with the portion farthest from the food in the morning and closest to the food in the evenings.

Back to the Foods

I've already discussed food sources and how they can help you to harvest a mature buck, and now we need to relate that to breeding behavior. During the rut you should take note that many open areas that do not attract bucks early in the season might do so once breeding begins. Bucks could move at any hour in search of a doe, and for some reason they don't mind looking over or occasionally crossing the open arenas. During the rut, an educated buck seems to possess the keen eyes of a pronghorn antelope.

Let's focus for a moment on ambush points for big bucks near fields when the breeding begins. These veterans usually have preferred arrival locations, like hillsides and hilltops, where visibility is best. In flat country, they usually arrive at the thickest locations, but an ambush site a few yards off an agricultural field can produce high dividends during the rut. Although super bucks seldom show up near fields in late mornings, they love to skirt fields along the fringes during the rut. Consider that a buck knows where does might have been through the night. He also knows that when the does left the field and entered the timber and thickets, they were sure to leave scent. He often travels the fringes just inside the timber to remain in cover, and will sometimes skirt the entire length of the field to pick up a doe's trail. For this reason, many trophy hunters don't mind hunting near fields during the rut. They also know that it could pay off at any time of the day.

Morning and Midday

Although I have taken several bucks in the evenings, and have enjoyed some midday action, when it comes to the rut I'm a morning lover. I'm not going to say that you should choose one or the other to hunt. In fact, the more often you are there, the better your chance of killing a super buck. However, mornings do seem to be the hottest for me when the rut is on. I believe most bucks simply refuse to stop feeding their libido when dawn arrives. They have been at it all night, and most bucks are calm. A few might even have gotten lucky. Most will not want to head into a bedding area at dawn, though, regardless of how lucky they were through the night.

Unlike hunting autumn mornings, the rut calls for long hours. Daylight might seem like the appropriate moment to shoot a big one, but there's just as much chance a whopper will walk past you several hours after sunrise. For this reason, always stick it out as long as possible.

If you can't hunt during midday but can hunt afternoons, arrive early. After a buck beds down sometime during the morning or midday period, he quickly becomes restless and anxious to get on the move. That's why midday hunting is so attractive during the rut. A buck needs but little rest before he moves again.

Midday ambush locations can be found near any place that attracts does and fawns. The key is to be there as long as possible and let the buck make a mistake. The more ground he covers, the better the chance you will see him. For midday hunting, I prefer ambush sites near isolated food sources, such as acorns, persimmons, and others. The travel corridors mentioned previously could produce action during midday, although they have worked best for me during mornings and evenings.

That brings up another point. Don't be afraid to make a move to another location as the day progresses. For example, if you hunt the fringes of a field, or perhaps a travel corridor in the morning, consider moving deeper into the timber or thickets a few hours later. Big bucks move during midday hours, but they are most likely to travel less and remain closer to a bedding area.

Another primary midday ambush site could be near a hot scrape or scrape line. I cover these areas extensively later in the book (see later in this chapter, and Chapter 5) and discuss those scrapes that provide the most potential. However, many veteran trophy hunters insist that the midday period of the rut is one of the best times to hunt a scrape. This is usually the case just days before the breeding begins.

You have an excellent opportunity to harvest a wall-hanger during the primary rut, but don't give up if you are unsuccessful. Some time later, another rut arrives for those who didn't get the job done the first time.

Secrets of the Second Rut

I've found that many hunters prefer not to hunt the second rut, although it provides an outstanding last-ditch effort to ambush a super buck. I also believe that most hunters naturally assume they have little chance of killing a big buck.

These hunters are sadly mistaken. True, finding and shooting the buck of your life might never become more than a second-rut fantasy. On the other hand, some die-hard hunters claim the hunting is positively fabulous during winter. Most of these positive individuals have absorbed two things. First, they have a sound understanding of the second rut, from what makes it tick to the methods used to intercept and surprise a huge buck. Second, they have a sound understanding of how deer move during winter and how weather is actually advantageous to the second-rut hunter.

To analyze the secrets of the second rut, let's first look at its ingredients. I would be a liar if I told you that you could anticipate its beginning with any real reliability following the peak rut. If we knew that, we wouldn't have to depend on extreme strategies to be successful. On the contrary, the timing of the second rut is anyone's guess. The primary rut, as we've seen, can usually be accurately determined within a few days, and there are plenty of reasons for this. Here's why the second rut is totally unpredictable.

Some hunters take for granted that the second rut will begin about one month after the first. They claim that the mature does that didn't breed during the peak rut will come into estrus again. I won't deny that a mature doe will come into estrus about twenty-eight days after her first estrus cycle (almost always occurs during the first rut), if she did not become pregnant. Nonetheless, a hunter would be unwise to believe there will be a few mature does available and ready to breed during the second rut. Nearly all mature does breed during the first estrus cycle. In fact, it's best if you believe it very rare for one not to breed during the peak rut. Bucks are on the move consistently once the breeding starts, and they aren't likely to miss finding a hot doe.

Because I hunt avidly through the muzzleloading and late archery seasons when the second rut typically occurs, I must believe that mature does have little or nothing to do with the beginning of the second rut. In all the years I've hunted, I recall witnessing only a handful of older does being pursued by a buck a month or so after the first rut. Nonetheless, that doesn't mean a second rut won't become a reality.

Second-Rut Fawns

With that said, we can move on to why and how the second rut works. Previously, I mentioned "beginning of the second rut." That statement is a bit misleading. You see, there isn't a beginning, at least not a noticeable one. You could assume it has started if you see one or more bucks in pursuit of a doe, but in fact the second rut might have begun earlier. It won't continue for a few days and then abruptly end, either. Unlike the first rut, the second rut is hit-and-miss. It could be hot one day, perhaps only two or three weeks after the peak rut, then become equally hot, or hotter three or four weeks later. In fact, you could spend several days in the field at prime time for the second rut, and never even notice it is underway.

The primary reason for the second rut is doe fawns. Some breed each year. Some don't breed until one year later during the peak rut. At any rate, fawns that do breed will not come into estrus at a particular time. Photoperiodism governs the timing of the first rut and when the mature does breed. However, fawns usually breed much later than mature does. One could come into estrus four to six weeks after the peak rut while another comes into estrus eight to twelve weeks after the mature does breed.

I have no idea just how many doe fawns come into estrus, nor am I aware of studies surrounding this behavior. I used to believe that about one fawn in five would breed their first season, but I've upped that figure in recent years to about one in three. I also believe that the earliest-born doe fawns are the healthiest, and more likely to breed than others. Those doe fawns born a few weeks after the first wave of births usually come from does that bred their first year, but late, during what we call the second rut. Unhealthy fawns probably don't breed their first year, despite when they are born. Mother Nature has a way of making sure that fawns in need of nutrition won't have to share it with an offspring.

Hot Second-Rut Ambush Locations

In many ways, hunting a big buck during the second rut doesn't differ from hunting one during the peak rut. It's usually best to plan your ambush where you expect the does to be, even though it will be the doe fawns attracting the big bucks. If hunting pressure has subsided for several days or weeks, and it usually has once doe fawns begin breeding, you can get away from trails and bedding areas, relying again on food sources. Be aware that food sources do change from autumn to winter, however. Then there are other ambush methods, such as finding and hunting new buck sign.

I don't put much emphasis on rubs and scrapes during the winter and second rut, but they do provide possibilities. Consider an Indiana ten-pointer I shot several years ago during the late archery season. He opened a new rub line a few weeks after the peak rut. I set up a stand along his route, within 100 yards of a probable bedding area. On the first morning, he traveled the trail of rubs within 20 yards of my tree stand. The buck that opened the rub line had probably returned to his home range after the peak rut ended. I felt fortunate to have been there when the buck followed the route, since I do most of my second-rut hunting near food sources.

Scrapes tend to die during the primary rut once the breeding begins, but scrapes that died earlier might suddenly come alive during the second rut. New scrapes can appear almost anywhere and everywhere during the primary rut, but new scrapes are uncommon during the second rut. A fresh scrape you find in the second rut is probably one that was there during the primary rut.

Many second-rut scrapes that become active are found along fringes of food-containing fields. Unfortunately, these scrapes die about as quickly as they become active. In other words, during the pre-rut period a scrape might remain active for a few weeks, whereas in the late season a scrape might be active for only a few days, and in some cases worked only once. I've found some scrapes that were hit once during the late season lay idle for a few weeks. However, these late-season idle scrapes often become active when a breeding doe fawn shows up and excites a buck.

Killing a big buck near a scrape in the second rut is tough business, simply because scrapes are not visited consistently as they once were. I've had far better success setting up near anything that's green.

The Greens

If you intend to plan your ambush near a food source, and you probably should if you hope to kill a big buck in the second rut, start by assuming that foods are more limited during the late season. In most areas, foods such as acorns, persimmons, apples, etc. have disappeared. For this reason, you should head for anything green. Granted, green vegetation is limited during late autumn and early winter when the second rut arrives, but that which remains could attract a mature buck.

In farmlands, most of the alfalfa, clover, and oats do not attract deer after several hard freezes. Temperature governs how well these fields will attract deer, and we know that cold temperatures take their toll quickly. However, winter wheat will attract all deer in many regions as other fields fail. There are also commercially produced seeds that can be sown to become active food plots for winter, particularly in areas lacking winter wheat.

I'm fortunate to hunt where winter wheat is somewhat abundant. I prefer small fields, simply because you can closely pinpoint the best ambush locations. Almost every late archery season, I see one or more whopper bucks in and around green fields. Sometimes it is due to a doe fawn nearing estrus that happens to come to the green field to feed. But, make no mistake, big bucks must eat heartily themselves. And what better place to do it, since a doe fawn could also be on the scene?

Natural vegetation such as honeysuckle and some types of brambles will also attract deer. Honeysuckle stays somewhat green throughout the year. It is not native to North America, but grows like wildfire in a summer drought in many regions. Some deer, moving little and preserving body heat, will stay close to honeysuckle thickets and seldom leave them during the late season.

If green foliage and fields are not available, most deer will turn to anything they can reach, even if it offers little nutrition. In some areas, I've spotted deer feeding in old harvested soybean fields, nipping the dried stubble that remains. If snow prevails, most deer will desert the fields and head for the thickets, where anything that is above the snow will immediately become an asset. Of course, this means the big bucks as well as the does are likely to be in the area.

A Lesson for the Second Rut

Although I would much rather plan my ambush near a green agricultural field for the second rut, deer often desert the fields after a few inches of snow. Some deer will paw down to reach the greens, but if other foliage above the ground is available, they probably won't work overtime.

Snow is advantageous for scouting during the late season and locating a super buck. Although serious scouting must usually prevail if you hope to learn where the deer are moving, and where a big buck might show, snow can help you to quickly discover the right ambush location.

Several years ago, my good friend Woody Williams used snow to his advantage to ambush a huge ten-pointer during the late season. He arrived early in the day, after a light snow had fallen the night before. His intentions were to locate fresh sign and the trails that provided the most promise. Woody understands the difficulty of late-season archery hunting, and that timing the second rut is hit-and-miss. Nevertheless, a short time later he located a hot trail and huge tracks penetrating the boundary of a dense pine thicket. The south end of the pine thicket connected to a narrow field that had attracted several deer in the area. He set up an ideal ambush location a short distance from the food source, hoping the bedding area of the pines would produce action. The action came shortly before dusk as a big buck ambled through the pines and approached his stand. A well-placed arrow put the buck down quickly.

No one can say whether the big tracks Woody discovered belonged to the mature buck he shot, but the possibility exists. It was a large-bodied buck, probably three-and-a-half years old. However, the successful hunter does know that the light snow and huge tracks he found played a decisive role in choosing this ambush location. Hunters are often tempted to hunt trails where they find the most tracks in snow, but this is not always the best choice when hunting a mature whitetail.

Keep in mind that if a light snow prevails and is on the ground for a few days, it often increases deer movement, improving scouting opportunities and upping the odds of a last-ditch effort to find and kill a big buck. A mature buck that might have moved very little when no snow was present might suddenly move consistently. That theory can change, though, when deep snow prevails, and the second rut winds down.

The Last Word on the Second-Rut Ambush

We can't deny the facts. By the time the peak rut ends, there aren't as many bucks roaming the woods, and the bulk of the harvest has occurred. Those that did survive the battle are not particularly anxious to move in daylight hours. The educated, mature bucks have wised up even more, and have allowed thoughts of breeding to dwindle.

Now the good news. Some old-timers have made it through yet another hunting season and will likely be around for the next hunting season.

CHAPTER 3

Big Buck Hot Spots and the Home-Range Factor

Serious trophy hunters agree on something that should be obvious: that you must hunt where big bucks exist. That's the first step to learning the habits of a big buck, and patterning his movements within his home range. Your woodsmanship and hunting abilities might enable you to see deer consistently anywhere you hunt, but your expertise won't produce a trophy whitetail if he's not there, or if you have not learned his whereabouts. Those who consistently bring home mature whitetails don't rely on happenstance to bring them to the right place at the right time. They make the ambush happen, and they begin with hunting where the possibility exists.

Hot Spots of the Record Books

The record books don't provide statistics of every big buck killed. Successful hunters may register their deer into the record books, and only a certain percentage of hunters do so. We therefore don't necessarily see the actual totals, but enough entries are made each year to see results, which tell us where a substantial percentage of the big bucks exist.

Before going on, let me emphasize one fact: big bucks are everywhere. They are not limited to certain areas of North America. Although some areas produce far more than others do, you have the opportunity to ambush a trophy whitetail close to home, even if it's hundreds of miles from a state or province that produces the bulk of monster whitetails.

There are states and provinces, however, that nevertheless consistently produce the largest Typical Whitetail bucks, as shown by records from the Boone and Crockett Club for the last ten years (see Tables 3-1, 3-2, and 3-3). For example, in 1995 Iowa led the way with thirty-seven entries, and almost always ranks in the Top Ten. In 2000 and 2004, Wisconsin produced the most entries. Many other states and provinces, such as Illinois, Missouri, Ohio, and Saskatchewan, also ranked in the Top Ten during 1995, 2000, and 2004.

Table 3-1: Top 10 Locations in the Typical category, Boone & Crockett Club, 1995

Rank	State/Province	Number of Entries
1	Iowa	37
2	Illinois	29
3	Wisconsin	25
4	Missouri	22
5	Kentucky	18
6	Kansas	16
7	Alberta	14
8	Indiana	14
9	Ohio	13
10	Saskatchewan	12

Table 3-2: Top 10 Locations in the Typical category, Boone & Crockett Club, 2000

Rank	State/Province	Number of Entries
1	Wisconsin	36
2	Iowa	28
3	Saskatchewan	27
4	Ohio	25
5	Illinois	24
6	Kentucky	24
7	Minnesota	18
8	Missouri	15
9	Alberta	12
10	Texas	10

Table 3-3: Top 10 Locations in the Typical category, Boone & Crockett Club, 2004

Rank	State/Province	Number of Entries
1	Wisconsin	21
2	Illinois	18
3	Ohio	13
4	Kentucky	11
5	Missouri	11
6	Iowa	9
7	Texas	9
8	Indiana	8
9	Kansas	8
10	Minnesota	7

Data of tables 3-1, 3-2, and 3-3 are from the Boone and Crockett Club's records database and are summarized in this book with the express written permission of the Boone and Crockett Club, 250 Station Drive, Missoula, MT 59801. To learn more about the club and the many activities it is involved in, please visit www.booneandcrockettclub.com or call 406-542-1888.

According to records of the Pope and Young Club, more than 23,000 whitetails were entered between 1989 and 2002. During this fourteen-year period, Wisconsin produced the most entries in the Typical Whitetail Category with 5,090. Illinois ranks second with 3,749, while third-ranked Iowa produced 2,177 Pope and Young bucks. The Top Ten states continue as: Ohio (1,634), Minnesota (1,557), Kansas (1,303), Michigan (952), Missouri (929), Indiana (920), and Texas (852).

Surprisingly, the number of entries has increased considerably in the Pope and Young Club in recent years. For example, during 2001–02, the club recorded 4,367, while in 1999–00, 4,176 bucks were entered. Jump back to 1995–96, and you see a significant difference: only 3,660 entries.

There are probably various reasons for the increase in numbers. We can speculate that interest in the club has increased, and there have been expanding whitetail populations. We also can't deny that many archers are veterans, and have become increasingly effective in hunting the whitetail.

I have compiled a table of Pope and Young Club entries showing the top areas from 1995 through 2002 for the entries include bucks that scored 150 or more, although the minimum score for entering a buck is 125 in the Typical category.

Table 3-4: Top 20 Locations for Pope & Young Entries Scoring 150 or more, 1995-2002

Rank	State/Province	Number of Entries
1	Illinois	599
2	Wisconsin	481
3	Iowa	370
4	Kansas	225
5	Ohio	191
6	Minnesota	110
7	Missouri	104
8	Indiana	102
9	Kentucky	71
10	Texas	67
11	Michigan	65
12	New York	61
13	Nebraska	57
14	Maryland	48
15	Pennsylvania	44

Rank	State/Province	Number of Entries
16	Alberta	39
17	West Virginia	33
18	South Dakota	30
19	Oklahoma	25
20	Colorado	17
20	Saskatchewan	17

Data of Table 3-4 are from the Bowhunting Records of North American White-tail Deer, Second Edition of the Pope and Young Club records database, and have been summarized in this book with the express written permission of Pope and Young Club, 273 Mill Creek Rd., P.O. Box 548, Chatfield, MN 55923. For more information about the club, visit www.pope-young.org or call 507-867-4144.

It is also important to understand that in some regions the best bucks come from isolated pockets of a particular state or province. In other words, it could be that most of a state's entries come from a few select counties or districts; perhaps the northern, central, or southern portion. Nevertheless, you can still bet that a big buck lurks close to your home.

I won't elaborate much on public versus private lands. I'm sure you are already aware that, in general, your chances of ambushing a super buck on private lands are much better than on public lands. There are exceptions, but these locales are scarce and usually areas that receive minimal hunting pressure. At the same time, some private lands fail to produce ambush opportunities due to extensive hunting pressure.

A 2003 study conducted by F+W Publications, publishers of *Deer & Deer Hunting Magazine,* showed that 87.3 percent of readers hunt private land. About 55 percent hunt public ground, while

26.8 percent spend their time on leased lands. The remaining percentage participate on Quality Deer Management lands.

The key difference between bucks that inhabit public lands and those dwelling on private lands is when they move. Because many deer on public lands might move close to dawn and dusk, becoming nearly nocturnal, the hunter might have to hunt harder and take more precautions to ambush a trophy buck. As I've said before, big bucks are seldom forgiving. The more hunters there are roaming about, the more a buck must forgive to roam the same area.

Home-Range Bucks

Shortly before writing this chapter, my good friend Tim Hilsmeyer called to say he had just spotted "Frankenstein." The buck earned his name the previous year after Tim had noted his distasteful appearance. The hunter saw the buck on numerous occasions the year before, and had passed shooting opportunities, waiting for a bigger one to appear. The antlers of Frankenstein were anything but normal. He was not a huge buck, but nonetheless had a rack that sported a weird main beam with erratic points, making him a potential target for the following season.

Tim spotted Frankenstein again in late summer just before the early archery season began the following year. The deer's antlers had grown but still lacked trophy quality. Tim was fortunate in that he hunts close to his home and has the opportunity to consistently monitor the nearby farmland areas. Each time he spotted

Frankenstein before the archery season opened, which Tim claims was no less than twenty times, the deer was feeding on soybeans. Moreover, like most bucks in late summer, the weird buck was on his own turf and home range. The deer had become quite dependable about visiting the same food sources and bedding areas. Tim continued to pattern Frankenstein and a couple of other bucks. Yet, while he had designated likely ambush locations within the buck's home range, Tim failed to see him during the hunting season. (Fortunately, Tim did cash in on another super buck before the archery season ended.) Tim's hunting area is not overrun with big bucks, but this nevertheless illustrates how many bucks stick to certain areas year after year during late summer and early autumn.

We can't deny that the peak rut offers the best ambushing opportunities when big bucks are covering ground. However, make no mistake, mature bucks do stick to tighter ranges and

Whether it be edge habitat typified by agricultural landscapes, or deep hardwoods, most bucks stick with their home ranges for most of the year.

can be patterned in autumn when confined to core areas. These bucks are somewhat vulnerable if the hunter can pattern them, set up strategically, and remain undetected. The key is to do it before the buck departs.

Home-Range Departures

When a buck expands his travel area, the hunter must resort to other tactics. The time a buck spends in his home range can vary. I've never been one to believe that a mature buck will roam over a great distance during the breeding cycle. Some do, but many don't. There are several questions that need to be considered: How close does a buck stay to his birth range throughout his life? How many big bucks widen their range as the rut approaches? Do mature bucks travel less than young bucks when the breeding begins? Will the number of available does play a role in the distance a buck disperses?

Studies have indicated that yearling bucks leave their home range at a much higher rate than mature bucks do, and at a higher rate than does of any age. The 1995 Stackpole book *Quality Whitetails* describes a 1992 study which showed that fifteen radio-collared male fawns, after thirty months of age, dispersed from their birth range. These were deer raised by does. Strangely, only 9 percent of orphan fawns that, for some reason or another, had lost their mother, left their home range. This could suggest that the dispersal of yearling bucks is influenced more by pressures of adult does than of bigger bucks.

With that said, we can reasonably conclude that a buck's home range might not always be in his birth area. A home range might be adapted thereafter. Nonetheless, the home range of any deer becomes "sacred ground"; a buck will rarely abandon it. The size of home range varies, but usually does not exceed one square mile. Habitat influences, climate, and disturbances can cause home range size to vary.

A study in Texas on the Welder Wildlife Refuge in 1965 (studies referenced here are published in *White-tailed Deer Ecology and Management*, Stackpole Books, 1984) indicated the home-range size of does ranged from 60 to 340 acres. Bucks utilized 240 to 880 acres. A Missouri study in 1958 showed that does had a home range of about 400 acres, and the home range of bucks neared 1,000 acres.

Range size expands for bucks when the breeding begins. One study showed that a Georgia buck added 400 acres to his range during the rut. It also showed that at the onset of the rut, six of nineteen bucks spread out an additional 2.8 miles from their previous range. Researchers noted that sexual competition among bucks caused the dispersal.

Young bucks probably roam farther than mature bucks. Approximately 10 percent of adult bucks left their home range at the Crab Orchard National Wildlife Refuge in Illinois in 1971. However, the same study indicated that about 80 percent of yearling bucks left their range. Being aware of this will certainly help the trophy hunter to ambush a big buck he knows is in the area. Some hunters will give up the pursuit of a certain buck when the rut arrives, believing he's departed the area. However, I can tell you that

I've seen several big bucks over the years that were in the same area during the rut that they were in during the pre-rut period.

Patterning Pre-Rut Bucks

Research provides hunters with valuable information, but a scientific approach does not always provide the methods you need for patterning and ambushing a trophy whitetail. Your success depends on how effectively you can pattern a buck without him knowing you are there.

Just how much stress a buck will take before he departs his home range remains a mystery. I've spooked some big bucks in their home range that were never spotted again. Perhaps they were still there. Perhaps they moved further away. However, I believe it best to assume that one mistake is capable of spoiling a future ambush. That's why patterning a big buck is serious business. Learning a buck's home range is not necessarily difficult if you have the time. Many hunters first learn the whereabouts of a big buck with a visual sighting.

Certain areas allow for easier sighting than in other areas, and agricultural terrain provides the best opportunities. In late summer and early autumn, as fields attract deer you can discover who's there. (See Chapter 1 for a discussion on foods and how they attract summer and autumn bucks.) An additional consideration is the importance of covering as much ground as possible to make visual sightings.

If roads provide access, grab your binoculars and drive often in early mornings and late afternoons to locate big bucks. This might seem a lazy way of scouting, but it's very effective. First, consider that spotting provides a positive ID, unlike sign that sometimes leaves you guessing whether a big buck was responsible. Second, consider that you don't have to penetrate the area and risk flushing a super buck into parts unknown. Finally, you can cover more ground in less time. The best news, though, is if you see a big buck, you will know where the hot spot exists and that you won't waste time hunting the wrong area.

Just how dependable a buck becomes will probably vary with the size of his home range. The smaller his range, the more likely it is for a hunter to see and pattern him. In the case of Frankenstein, the buck visited the same late-summer field often in the evenings, which suggested the buck might have had a small home range. Tim usually saw the buck about thirty minutes before dusk. There were times when he arrived earlier or later, and times when he didn't show at all, but Tim nevertheless considered this buck dependable. Some bucks won't be as dependable as Frankenstein, and you shouldn't believe that any buck will show in the same location each day. However, spotting a buck more than once in any given area could indicate a buck is within his home range and provides a patterning opportunity.

Regardless of whether you make a visual sighting or not, the time comes when you must walk into a buck's home range. Visual sightings near roads might provide evening ambush possibilities near food sources, but they won't provide ambush opportunities within the buck's core area.

I often rely upon early-season rub lines for ambush sites. These are primary targets for trophy hunters before the peak rut (more on this in Chapter 5). However, bedding areas and trails are also principal sites for patterning and ambushing a mature buck.

Always assume that for the pre-rut period, a big buck is often a creature of habit. He travels less than he does when breeding begins. The less distance he travels, the easier you can find his trails and bedding areas.

Before breeding begins, big bucks tend to stick to secondary trails. These trails do not indicate signs of heavy usage, such as primary trails that are often laced with droppings and tracks, courtesy of the greater traffic—does, fawns, small bucks—traveling them. Secondary trails are more difficult to locate due to less sign. It's also true that these trails often intercept primary trails.

Consider one such trail in an area I hunt. My wife Vikki and I call this trail "Big Buck Ridge." It's a primary trail traveling east-to-west, but a secondary trail that crosses it and travels north-to-south shows far less usage. However, the trail location earned its title only because we've spotted several big bucks traveling the secondary trail.

That's not to say that every secondary trail is a big-buck magnet, however. Some are, and others don't. In the case of Big Buck Ridge, this trail winds through a thicker area than the primary trail it crosses. It also links to dense undergrowth about 100 yards away, which obviously serves as a bedding area. Even better, it's quite common to find an early-season rub line along the trail. To locate the best secondary trails in your area, look for those that link with the thickest areas. Rubs may or may not be present, but they certainly add hope to the ambush.

It's worth reviewing the risks of penetrating a mature buck's range. Keep in mind that you could spoil your hunt before it begins. For this reason, always do your scouting and set up ambush sites when bucks are not likely to be moving. Windy days provide the best opportunities. Finally, avoid walking into potential bedding areas. I never follow a secondary trail for a long distance — just far enough to find a suitable ambush location. It's much better to set up too far from the best spot than to send the buck you hunt into parts unknown.

Return of the Survivors

We know that a mature buck probably won't expand his range until breeding is close. Once the rut kicks in, he could still be in the same vicinity, or he could be a mile or more away. It's also true that he might or might not survive the rut.

Once the breeding winds down, most surviving bucks return to their home range — the same area they depended upon during the pre-rut period. Availability of food and cover might cause an expansion of the buck's home range, however. I base this theory upon my findings, as well as those of other avid hunters who stick with it until the bitter end.

Several years ago, Indiana hunter Dean Stallion spotted a massive-antlered buck chasing a doe during the muzzleloader season. This was a few weeks after the first rut. Although the hunter hoped this was the buck's home range, he began to have doubts. Dean failed to see the monster buck for the remainder of the muzzleloader and late archery season. In fact, many months later he had nearly forgotten about the buck. However, three weeks into the archery season the following year, during the pre-rut stage, he was rewarded as the buck left a bedding area and came to a water hole. Dean's arrow put the buck down quickly, and the huge deer taped out at 189 inches.

This case suggests that a mature whitetail might return to its home range after the primary rut. Or, perhaps, Dean's buck never ventured far from his home range during the rut. One thing we do know: the buck was obviously in his home range after the peak rut one year, and before the peak rut the next year.

There seems to be plenty of research that indicates the number of bucks dispersing during the rut, but we don't find many answers about bucks returning to their home range after the rut. Occasionally, I see the same buck after the breeding subsides in the same range that I saw him during the pre-rut period. In other words, the only time I didn't see the buck was during the breeding cycle—the short period when the buck ventured away from his home range in search of estrous does.

Of course, some bucks don't return to their home range after breeding ends. Cases in which sightings are uncommon are probably contingent upon survival rates of older bucks. Simply said, many don't return because they were killed during the rut. However, if you are looking to ambush the same big buck you patterned during the pre-rut period, your best bet might be to return to the buck's home range when the late season arrives and the second rut becomes a factor.

Few parameters are carved in stone when it comes to a mature buck's home range, but you can bet that every buck has one and will depend upon it at least for a period. It's sometimes difficult to determine when he will be there and even more difficult to learn his next move. Nonetheless, it's possible to pattern the right buck and kill him before or after the rut.

Awareness of a big buck's existence could be the most important factor to ambushing him. Although it takes time and effort to locate a big one, it saves you time in the end. You can spend countless hours waiting to ambush a trophy whitetail in an area where a trophy whitetail won't arrive until the peak of the rut, or perhaps not arrive at all. If, however, you know he's in the area, you are not wasting time. Each time you hunt, the possibility exists that he could walk past you.

CHAPTER 4

Spicing Up the Ambush Site:
Smell Right, Sound Good

I have said throughout this book that you must make things happen to ambush a super whitetail. That is accomplished by hunting smart and applying advanced ambush tactics. Nevertheless, you do have an ace in the hole. Calls and scents could lure a whopper buck in close when other tactics barely miss. In other words, you might be in the right ambush location to intercept a big buck, yet he could pass by without you knowing, or perhaps stop just beyond effective shooting range.

First, let me express my opinion of calls and scents, and why they might or might not help you to ambush a buck. They should never be treated haphazardly, nor regarded as a full-time hunting method. Mature whitetails are not fooled easily, and you are better off using calls and scents as a backup method. I've taken a few respectable bucks with their help, but it's not because I walked into the woods with the idea that these lures would make the difference. There are right times to use calls and scents, but these days are few and far between.

When Grunts Lure in
Trophy Whitetails

This section does not get into the basics of deer calls, such as types of calls and mastering calls. That's irrelevant, since manufacturers have perfected deer sounds. It takes but little practice for the hunter to perfect a call. The importance lies in when and how you attempt to lure a big buck in close.

The grunt tube is the most popular call, and rightfully so, as both young and old bucks grunt. Some call manufacturers have made grunt tubes intended to sound like a yearling, and others like a mature buck, but I can't really say there is a major difference between the tone of young and old bucks. I also have found that any grunt sound can lure in a mature buck on the right day.

The idea of grunting is to make the big buck believe that another buck is at your ambush location. Consider a huge eight-pointer that I shot with a bow, just three years before writing this chapter. He followed the side of a ridge about 80 yards from my tree stand. After three grunts, the buck slicked back his ears, apparently angry, and rapidly closed ground. Moments later, I shot the buck at 10 yards. He was obviously ready to respond upon hearing the grunts, and precisely zeroed in on the place from which the sound came.

I have had the best results with grunts at the onset of the breeding period, and continuing from two weeks before the breeding begins until the post-rut era begins. However, I carry a grunt tube with me throughout the hunting season, beginning during the archery season at the earliest part of the pre-rut period.

High-volume grunt calls are necessary. Some calls have it and some don't. Keep in mind that it's easy to tone a call down with your hand, or by blowing softer, but you can't make a low-volume call louder. Many hunters do not enjoy success with a grunt call because a passing buck doesn't hear it. The range of a call often depends upon wind, how much noise the buck is making as he walks, and the volume of the call. The eight-pointer I just mentioned did not hear my first grunt. That's why I had to grunt a second time. Upon hearing that grunt, he stopped. The final grunt was to allow him to pinpoint my location. I would suggest that you grunt no more than necessary. Once you have a buck's attention, grunt again so he knows exactly where you are. The next move should be up to him.

Some hunters claim they grunt to a buck, only to see the deer keep moving and pay no attention to the call. In all reality, the buck probably didn't hear the grunt. Most any buck, big or little, usually shows some reaction. For this reason, I recommend that you never assume a buck is uninterested. Even if he doesn't come to the call, he will usually stop. If he doesn't stop, he probably did not hear it.

One exception to this reasoning is if he is already in pursuit of a doe. In other words, if he has visual contact with a doe ahead of him, or if she is right in front of him, he will not leave the doe to check out your grunts. As they say, a bird in the hand is worth two in the bush. Nevertheless, if he's trailing a hot doe and he doesn't know exactly where she is, he might very well respond to a grunt, believing another buck is already with her.

Several years ago, I watched a two-and-a-half-year-old buck in hot pursuit of a doe until they disappeared over a hill. In the

When responding to a grunt call, a buck will not circle and come towards you with the wind in his face – if he's interested, he will come almost immediately.

meantime, the doe's fawn remained under my tree feeding on acorns. A short time later, the buck came back with his nose on the ground, attempting to find the doe. Apparently, he had lost her. Thus, I took advantage of the situation and grunted. He came in immediately, and within seconds my arrow zipped through the buck's vitals.

Two factors helped me to harvest this buck. First, the buck probably thought upon hearing the grunts that another had joined in the pursuit of the hot doe, and he wasn't about to let another buck get in on the action. Second, I believe the fawn nearby helped. The buck had spotted it and came directly toward it, as if to think the button buck had done the grunting.

Anytime you have a non-target deer close, it's a good time to grunt at a passing buck. A big buck doesn't like any other bucks grunting. In fact, that's exactly why big bucks respond more to grunts than do little bucks. Any other deer around is like a live decoy. It seems they can't help but to react after they hear the grunts and see the deer.

I would avoid grunting to a super buck that is accompanied by a doe. He won't respond. A big buck isn't likely to leave a doe to investigate a source he cannot see. It's also true that a big buck couldn't care less about another buck when he already has what he wants. Grunting to him could alert the doe and cause concern. By not grunting, the possibility exists that the buck and doe could eventually come toward you. When a mature buck pursues a doe that isn't quite ready, anything could happen. She could change directions a dozen times in a short period. One moment she might be walking away, and the next she could advance directly toward you.

Bowhunters are often tempted to grunt when they see a buck close, barely beyond bow range. However, a buck that is perhaps only 50 yards from your ambush site can usually pinpoint the call and determine that another buck is not present. I would therefore suggest you call only if the buck is well beyond your effective shooting range. One exception could be if you are in extremely dense cover. This could force the buck to hunt for you, which is exactly what you want to do when calling to a buck.

Keep in mind that bucks will not circle you and come in with the wind in their nose upon hearing a grunt. If they respond to a grunt, most will instinctively and immediately come toward you.

For this reason, calling to a buck that is downwind could be the worst thing you could do, and one sure way of further educating an already educated buck.

Finally, I suggest you do not fall victim to random calling. Random calling could be defined as grunting every so often while on stand. This method seldom works. A buck isn't likely to hear your call if it's not in view, and it could even send up a red flag to one that does hear the call. Who's to say a big buck wasn't already coming toward you before you called? As mentioned previously, save your grunts for the big bucks you can see and that you know will not come closer.

Table 4-1: Trout's Eight Rules for Calling Bucks

1	Don't call to a downwind buck
2	Always use a call capable of high volume
3	Never assume a buck is uninterested
4	Avoid calling to a buck coming towards you
5	Don't call to a buck that is close
6	Avoid calling to a buck that is accompanied by a doe
7	Limit random calling
8	Always believe a buck's personality could change

Rattling Techniques

Rattling antlers together to attract a mature buck is nothing new. However, many hunters are still unaware of how and when it should be done for the best results.

Consider that rattling is most likely to fool a big buck late in the pre-rut period, just before the breeding begins. Yearling bucks tend to spar more often than trophy bucks, and usually two to four weeks before the peak rut. Big bucks often don't care about sparring long before breeding begins, but battles between big bucks can occur just before breeding. This is also the time when territorial disputes arise.

Although the timing of your rattling might be on target, I would suggest you avoid rattling too much. A mature buck could become suspicious if he hears consistent rattling. I prefer to rattle in three sequences. Each sequence should last about a minute, with a few minutes gap between each. Also, consider that rattling is an option to make something happen if your ambush location has not paid off. It should not become a daily strategy.

When mature bucks fight, it's rare and serious business, usually close to the time does are about to breed, and this is the time when rattling comes into its own.

Rattling works best during the pre-rut period as bucks settle disputes.

I took a huge Alberta whitetail in 1990 on the last evening of a weeklong hunt, right before dusk, and just days before the peak rut. Several factors led up to the harvest (which you'll read about in Section II). I mention this deer now, though, to illustrate that rattling can pay off when other tactics fail.

Although grunting should be used when a big buck might not come closer, you could consider random rattling throughout your hunt. Personally, I keep rattling on the back burner. I prefer to let my tactical ambush strategies do the job, and rattle only during an occasional hunt late in the pre-rut.

When Scents Count

The scent business has grown immensely in recent years. Using scents is nothing new; trappers have relied on scents since trapping first came to be. There's still plenty we don't know about scents, but the one thing we do know is that sometimes they work and sometimes they don't.

There are different scents, from those that mask human scent, to those that arouse curiosity and actually lure the buck to you. The question is, do scents fool a mature buck?

I'm not going to elaborate on some scents. For instance, let me point out that no masking scent can completely cover human scent when conditions are very unfavorable. Unfavorable conditions are when a buck approaches downwind of the hunter. You can apply large quantities of masking scents, or you can wear scent-eliminating clothing, but nothing fools a big buck's nose when he faces into the wind.

I do believe lure scents could help the trophy hunter to ambush a noteworthy buck, providing the hunter uses the right scent on the right day. First, the lures should be fresh to provide the best results. Some scent companies get their scents from live deer, while others manufacture their scent to smell like the real thing. I don't know if one is better than the other. I've seen deer respond negatively and positively to both. As for how one responds negatively, let me just say that I've seen deer smell some scents, then turn and walk away.

The right day for a lure to work is dependent upon the type of lure, and how and when it is used. There are all kinds of lures, from food smells, to doe-in-estrus scents, to deer urine. I'm not going into food scents, either. These scents could attract a trophy whitetail, or a doe fawn, or nothing at all. However, I will discuss sex lures and which days they have the best chance of luring in a mature buck.

Many hunters consider scrapes as sacred ground, and rightfully so. In fact, in using scents, I believe those used at natural existing scent locations, such as scrapes, provide the most potential. Although many hunters also believe it's the urine in the scrape that means the most, this is not necessarily the case. In fact, research has shown that it's the limb above the scrape that is licked, and often rubbed by the forehead gland, that is most important. Yet this doesn't necessarily mean that you shouldn't use scent on the ground. In fact, it might be more advantageous to apply scent both on and above the scrape.

As you will read in the following chapter, it's often the preferred scrapes that offer the best opportunities for an ambush. This is why I limit my scent applications to scrapes that occur in the same locations year after year, and to scrapes located in strategic locations.

Some hunters use scent trails, which consist of sex lures and/or urines. However, I would suggest you not lay a scent trail while wearing leather boots. Big bucks are not going to be fooled by a lure that coexists with human scent. Always wear rubber boots to eliminate as much human scent as possible, and avoid laying a trail through high weeds since your clothing also will leave scent along the trail.

Boot pads and drags make it possible to place a scent trail on the side of your walking trail. However, you must make certain that the trail gets hotter and not colder as it nears your ambush location. This can be accomplished by adding scent to the pad every few yards. If you add scent only when you begin walking toward your ambush site, the trail will weaken as it gets closer to the site. If a buck does pick up the trail, he could end up following it the wrong direction.

Hunters often soak bootpads or use scent
drags to lure a buck into range. Always make
certain the trail gets hotter, not colder, as it
nears your ambush location.

Another mistake often made is the distance of the scent trail.
I would suggest you rely on a trail 100 to 200 yards long. The idea
is to pick up a buck as he crosses the scent trail, and entice him
to follow it to you. The farther the buck has to travel to get to you,
the better the chance something will go wrong.

One other scent tactic is to place canisters or wicks around
your ambush location. Personally, I've never enjoyed success
using this method, but others claim it has provided positive results. I'm not so sure scent around you will attract a buck from any

great distance, however. I've found a buck must be close before it picks up the scent. In fact, I believe scents perform positively only when a buck makes contact with the scent at a short distance. Scent might help a bowhunter achieve the right shot, but don't count on it to bring a buck in from parts unknown. Strangely, a buck can smell a human at a considerable distance when conditions are favorable, but I've yet to see a buck respond to a lure at such distances.

I would never suggest you use scents consistently. I also believe they are best used when your ambush locations are not paying off. After all, you could miss seeing a super whitetail only because he's a short distance away. I recommend you save scents for the breeding period, when big bucks look for the scent trail of a doe or another buck, or when he visits the hottest scrape in the area.

CHAPTER 5

Reading Rubs and Scrapes: *How to Profile a Big Buck Based on His Sign, and How This Influences the Ambush*

R ubs and scrapes are perhaps the most notable buck sign found throughout the hunting season. Many hunters plan their ambush around rubs and scrapes. Yet I would suspect that more bucks meet their demise near food sources and trails than at signposts. That's not to say that rubs and scrapes don't offer potential. On the contrary, I sincerely believe that certain signposts can set the stage for ambushing a mature whitetail, providing your timing is correct when planning the ambush near rubs and scrapes, and providing you recognize those that offer the most potential.

We are still learning the true nature of rubs. Hunters have done their best to evaluate rubs, and determine those that offer ambush possibilities. Research also has helped to explain why bucks rub, the types of trees bucks prefer to rub, and when rubbing is most likely to occur. However, the jury is still out when it comes to the real meaning of buck rubs.

As antlers harden in late summer, a buck's hormones begin to change. The pre-rut is on, once the antlers have lost their velvet.

Several years ago, a writer reported that rubs show you only where a buck has been, and that scrapes show you where a buck will soon be. I disagree with that theory. In fact, I've had far more success and sightings hunting the best rubs than the best scrapes. Granted, it's not always easy knowing which rubs are likely to produce the action, but bucks do return to certain rubs. Keep in mind, the hottest scrape action occurs during the onset of the breeding cycle, when bucks are least predictable. Rubs, on the other hand, begin early when a buck is in his home range, and continue throughout the peak rut and the weeks following the breeding cycle. Rub activity often decreases after the rut, but does not diminish entirely.

Rub Research

When bucks rub trees, they leave scent from their forehead gland for all other deer to notice. Oftentimes, a buck batters the lower part of a tree, then gently rubs forehead scent above the rubbed area along the tree trunk and/or on branches. However, the scent of the forehead gland (appearing as a black patch between the antlers) becomes more active during the breeding season.

Rubbing begins once the velvet is gone from the antlers and intensifies in the following weeks. Some trees are rubbed by more than one buck.

When bucks approach a rubbed tree, they often smell the tree in what appears to be an effort to know who has been there. This is probably one reason why bucks prefer to rub aromatic trees, such as pine, cedar, and maples.

More than one buck may rub the same tree, and even does have been observed scenting and licking a previously rubbed tree. We can thus assume that all deer take this signpost seriously. Observers have noted that scent left on rubs can remain for several days when conditions are favorable. The signpost itself often remains bright and appears somewhat fresh for months.

The more mature bucks there are in the area, the more rubs you will find. In the 1980s, researchers noticed 5,000 rubs per square mile on the Mount Holly Plantation in South Carolina. Yet, on areas where bucks are heavily harvested, rub density ranged from 500 to 1,500 per square mile.

Although rub research provides some answers, it does little to help us ambush a trophy buck. There are still plenty of questions to be answered—from knowing whether a big buck is responsible for rubs, to knowing where and when to hunt rubs for the best results.

Big Rubs versus Little Rubs

One buck can rub hundreds of trees, from the time it begins in late summer until it sheds antlers during winter. A small buck could rub the same tree that was previously hit by a large buck. The more times a tree is rubbed, the more damage it receives and the more it looks like only a big buck is responsible.

It's also true that big bucks rub little trees, and little bucks rub big trees. I've often observed one-and-a-half-year-old bucks rubbing trees with a diameter of three to four inches. By the same token, I've spotted trophy bucks rubbing small, one-inch saplings. Mature bucks tend to cause distinct damage to trees, however. When determining the size of the buck that left the rub, I put more emphasis on damage than girth of the tree.

When inspecting the trunk of the tree, look for deeply gouged streaks. Heavy bucks with large antlers typically leave distinctive lines cut into the trunk. Equally important is the damage to limbs and the trunk of the tree. Some small saplings are often broken in half, and many large-diameter trees will display broken limbs above the primary rub if a mature whitetail is responsible.

Nevertheless, a big buck doesn't demolish every tree it rubs. For this reason, we can't assume a big buck is absent from the area if we locate only small rubbed trees with no major damage. What matters most is whether you can locate a rub line.

Sporadic Rubs versus Rub Lines

Locating rubs is seldom difficult. You can usually find rubs with little effort almost anywhere—along trails, near food sources, and close to bedding areas. However, rubs that you locate here and there that do not connect from one to another are considered sporadic rubs. These individual rubs seldom provide an ambushing opportunity. Continuous rubs that appear to follow a distinct course provide evidence of a rub line, and demonstrate a buck's previous travel route. Better yet, a rub line indicates a buck might travel the route again.

You can count on finding far more sporadic rubs than rub lines. I couldn't begin to tell you how many sporadic rubs I located last season alone in my primary hunting area. There were hundreds, and the only ones that I considered to offer an ambush opportunity were those near some food sources. As discussed in previous chapters, some foods often attract bucks before the rut as they come to feed. Even as the rut progresses, bucks visit hot foods to search for does. Rubs are typically found near these foods, and even if they seldom tie into a rub line, they do let you know a buck could return.

Because foliage begins diminishing in late autumn, rub lines are found more readily as the season progresses. Rub lines are not as promising for the trophy hunter just before and during the breeding cycle, however. In fact, the timing couldn't be worse. Once a buck begins widening his area in search of does, he seldom travels the rub lines of his home range.

Rub lines are primarily home-range signposts. They provide the most potential in early autumn through the pre-rut period, and perhaps during post rut when bucks again visit their home range. I consistently rely on locating rub lines each year in early autumn at the onset of the archery season, since a buck might travel it regularly. That's not to say, though, that you can count on action the first time you set up near a rub line. No buck is that dependable. However, if you have located a rub line long before the rut, there's a good chance your efforts will pay off. A few years ago, I held to a particular rub line during the first three weeks of the archery season, making it a point to be there as long as the wind was favorable. I hunted the location about six times, spotting two different bucks following the route.

Nothing is carved in stone when it comes to the number of rubs along a rub line, and the distance between rubs. Sometimes you can visually follow one rub to another. For instance, of the rub line previously mentioned, most rubs were about 30 to 50 yards apart.

Most rub lines appear along trails, but these are seldom well-used routes. In fact, you will usually notice the rubs before the trails. I would suggest, though, that you walk certain areas both coming and going, since you might see some rubs only when you walk in a particular direction. It's easy to miss rubs when you walk through an area only once.

Many believe that you can determine the direction in which a buck is traveling by the location of the rub. In other words, some

Author inspects a rub. Although many believe that large bucks rub large trees and smaller bucks rub smaller trees, the opposite can often be true.

hunters claim the rub will face into the direction a buck travels. I'm not so sure about that, however. Bucks often move around a tree, choosing a likely spot to rub. Then, they turn around and continue in the same direction they were moving when they approached the tree.

When you do locate a rub line, follow it in both directions. Because many lead to and from bedding areas, I would suggest you use extreme caution, making certain you do not penetrate the bedding area.

Rub lines appear most often near the thickest cover. Funnels, fencelines, and other natural travel corridors are also likely areas for locating rub lines. In contrast, the fringes of agricultural lands and large pockets of open hardwoods are not ideal locations. You can usually locate sporadic rubs in these areas, but seldom will they provide evidence of a rub line.

The distance of a rub line also varies. Some are visible for only 150 yards or less, while others might be followed for 300 or more yards. Most rub lines I locate and hunt cover a distance of 100 to 200 yards. Last year's rub line was short, and no more than 125 yards long. The rubs bordered a dense thicket (probably the bedding area), and continued through brush and hardwoods for a short distance before coming to a halt.

It helps if you can determine the freshness of a rub. Any rub line found in early autumn is likely to be fresh, but as the season progresses, a rub line could become deserted. Experience is the solution to analyzing rubs. The more rubs you examine, the better you get at determining those that were made in recent days. Loose strands of bark under the tree do not necessarily indicate a fresh rub, as bark can remain at the base of a tree for a long time.

It also will help if you keep an eye on the rub line—new rubs might appear if a buck or bucks continue using the route.

Some rub lines might appear in the same vicinity season after season, which indicates a buck might prefer using the same route and rub line. Oftentimes, when following a rub line in early autumn, I locate dark rubs and scarred trees (both live and dead trees). These old rubs could be from the previous year, or perhaps from preceding years. Some are only in the vicinity of the new rubs, while other old rub lines follow the same route as the new rub line.

Unlike scrapes to which a buck might return, bucks don't make it a point to visit a rubbed tree so they can rub it again. That's why sporadic rubs seldom provide ambushing opportunities. Bucks do follow rub lines with some consistency because it is a preferred travel route. Unfortunately, rub lines are active only when a buck is in his home range.

It's always tempting to hunt rubs and rub lines. This distinctive sign is readily found and hard to pass up, but you must resort to other tactics as the breeding cycle accelerates. When does are in the limelight, a buck's route and his scrapes could provide the better ambush.

Big Bucks and Scrape Facts

Like most avid hunters, I thoroughly enjoy locating a fresh scrape. However, rest assured that finding a hot scrape does not necessarily mean it will produce a super whitetail. On the contrary, most often the greatest reward you may get from a scrape is the excitement that it causes. Scrapes are probably less dependable than certain food sources, trails, and even rub lines. Some hunters do enjoy success hunting over a scrape or scrape line, but I'm not so sure that you should consider them the best sign for ambushing a big buck.

The timing in finding and hunting scrapes is vital to success, as are the types of scrapes you locate. In other words, hunting over a scrape at the wrong time could waste time. Researchers have learned a great deal about scrapes, but they have not determined that scrapes provide a guarantee that any buck will return, much less one that is a trophy candidate. Of course, there are no guarantees you will ambush a mature whitetail regardless of any sign you locate, or your expertise in the field. Scrape hunting provides some potential, and hunters should consider it an effective tactic, but I would not suggest it be your primary tactic. Here's how it could work for you.

Science of Scrapes

While scraping is a result of photoperiodism and rut activity, it is not limited to the breeding period. Bucks often begin scraping in late summer and early autumn once the velvet is removed from their antlers. Just how early you will locate scrapes might depend on the number of bucks in the area. Scrapes seldom show up until a few weeks before the breeding begins in areas with a low buck-to-doe ratio. If the area has a high buck-to-doe ratio, you are likely to discover scrapes in early fall. However, these scrapes are usually found near fringes of fields and serve as boundary scrapes. They provide proof of a buck's existence, but they do not provide a direct hunting opportunity for a big buck.

Big versus Little versus Recurring Scrapes

Each season, I locate scrapes of various sizes. Some are no larger than a typical turkey scratching. Most are at least three feet in diameter. A selected few will become as large as the hood of a vehicle. Although the biggest scrapes will probably excite you the most, I would not suggest you limit your attempts to ambush a buck near a large scrape.

Over the years, a few writers and hunters have categorized scrapes and claimed that the larger signposts should be noted as primary scrapes that offer the best ambushing opportunities. I've never found that the case. Big scrapes look more impressive, but that's as far as it goes. More emphasis should be placed upon recurring scrapes. In other words, those that show up in the same locations each season, regardless of their size, will provide the best results.

Consider Zeke, a buck my wife and I named a few years ago. The eight-pointer commonly visited the same scrape for two years in a row. It was your typical boundary scrape, located along a narrow winter wheat field under a post oak tree. We could never set up a tree stand near the post oak due to a lack of large trees, but we did set up a short distance away. The buck visited the scrape more than once each year in the evenings, usually just before dusk. He would always refresh the scrape and rub his forehead on the overhanging limbs.

We are unsure if Zeke is still in the area, but the scrape continues to be active each year, earning the title of a recurring scrape. It is usually opened about three weeks before the breeding begins, and remains active for a few weeks following the first breeding cycle.

Many years ago, I found a scrape in an area of thickets and hunted it whenever the wind was favorable. This went on for three years until the area was eventually cleared for farming. Each season, though, the scrape became hot. I never took a buck at the scrape, but did see several different bucks visit it throughout the breeding period. Again, we can label it as a recurring scrape and one that could attract a mature buck.

I do believe, as do many trophy hunters, that recurring scrapes will provide you with the best opportunity of ambushing a mature buck near a scrape. For this reason, always pay close attention to the location of scrapes you find during the hunting season. What you find one season could be hot the next.

Each year after the hunting ends, I often use the inactive winter months for shed hunting and scouting for old rubs and scrapes. I will discuss these tactics later, but mention it now to let you know that old scrapes are easily found after the foliage has dwindled. That's not to say that old scrapes you find are recurring scrapes, but at least you know where they are and can check them as the breeding nears in the upcoming season. If one or more become active, you can assume the scrape may attract a big buck.

Any scrape that is visited each year provides potential to ambush a super buck. There has to be a good reason that some bucks prefer to scrape the same location each year. Perhaps the repeated urine scent in the soil is a factor? The overhanging limbs are obviously a factor. Every recurring scrape I have found has always included overhanging limbs that bucks use to rub glands, lick, or chew.

I should add that no recurring scrape attracts only big bucks or little bucks. Mature whitetails do not necessarily guard an active recurring scrape. If the scrape is hot and frequently hit, it is certainly a scrape to hunt for a big buck. Little bucks might also visit the scrape, but what counts is that the scrape has been active more than one hunting season.

Scrapes found under trees often produce the best opportunities for an ambush. Overhanging limbs above the scrape are important to all deer that visit it. A buck often rubs his forehead gland on the limb, or chews and/or licks the limb.

When attempting to ambush a super buck, I prefer setting up as close as possible to the recurring scrape. You could ambush a buck en route, but you easily miss the action by setting up along a trail that leads to the scrape. Similar to the isolated foods discussed previously, a scrape should be considered the final destination and the primary reason a big buck will be there. You never know the route he will use to get there, nor do you know the trail he will use when he leaves, but you do know the scrape is where he will arrive.

Recurring scrapes can show up anywhere, but those that are located in dense areas tend to provide the greatest potential. I would avoid penetrating extremely thick areas since these could harbor a buck during daylight hours. Recurring scrapes along the fringes of thickets should be considered extremely valuable to a buck, primarily because he doesn't have to travel far from his security zone to check it.

Scrape Lines

Scrapes are similar to rubs, in that both provide important sign-post information for all deer. Moreover, for the hunter a scrape line could be more important than one scrape, just as a rub line provides more opportunity than sporadic rubs.

Unlike the individual scrape that might attract a buck, a scrape line usually occurs along certain trails leading to and from bedding areas and food sources. The bucks already know that does use the trail, and fully realize that a scrape along the trail could contain the scent of doe urine.

I don't believe that scrape lines are freshened as often as individual recurring scrapes, but I do believe that big bucks visit them consistently in search of does as the breeding accelerates. With this in mind, we can assume that most scrape lines don't become apparent until the onset of the rut, and usually appear along travel routes. Funnels, fencelines, and similar travel corridors are particularly attractive to bucks opening scrape lines during the rut. We can also assume that scrape lines are often more effective for the hunter at the onset of breeding, whereas recurring scrapes appear most active two or three weeks before the rut peaks.

Although scrape lines might not be freshened as often as some individual scrapes, it does appear that many scrape lines are hit shortly after rain. It seems likely that when a buck passes each scrape and doesn't detect scent, he may be compelled to freshen it and leave scent.

For this reason, I believe that scrape lines offer the best opportunities after rain, but I hunt scrape lines when I find them, regardless of rain-removed scent. However, I believe bucks take scrape lines very seriously at the onset of breeding and will almost always make it a point to travel the line just before does come into estrus, or just after the breeding begins.

A scrape line could contain numerous scrapes, or perhaps only a handful. The trails that host them are usually preferred, and used actively, by does. The trail could lead to a food source or bedding area, and it could require extensive searching of trails to locate one that has become a scrape line.

Distance between scrapes can vary from a few yards to a considerable distance. Most scrape lines I've located show evidence of scrapes about 20 to 75 yards apart. In some cases, the scrapes could be widespread and not tied into a scrape line. In fact, this is one problem with locating a hot scrape line. You have to walk trails thoroughly, and you risk spooking the big buck that could show up tomorrow. If I locate three to six scrapes along the same trail, I forgo looking further. I already have the evidence I need to plan the ambush, and I don't want to risk flushing any bucks in the vicinity.

Although it might be difficult to determine the best place to set up along a trail, since you might not know the direction from which a buck will come to visit the scrapes, I suggest you use common sense. Hunt close to the scrape line and set up only where the wind blows your scent away from the trail.

When it comes to recurring scrapes, scent is probably the greatest determining factor for a buck revisiting a precise location, before and during the breeding cycle. When it comes to a scrape line, scent is also important. However, the line attracts bucks most during the rut because they know it is located along a primary travel route used by does.

Synthetic Scrapes

Man-made scrapes, usually referred to as "mock scrapes," have become popular in recent years. Scent companies now provide an array of sex lures and gadgets for dispensing scents on scrapes. Some hunters don't make their own scrapes, but rely on freshening an existing scrape periodically to keep it alive. Do these tactics work?

I have never taken a buck over a synthetic scrape, or at an existing scrape I have freshened with lures. Nor have I witnessed a mature buck visit a scrape I have worked. In each case, though, I have found them freshened by bucks during the off-hours when I wasn't there. Additionally, some hunters have claimed that refreshing an existing scrape or a mock scrape works wonders when conditions are favorable and the proper methods are applied.

Modern scents and dispensers have made it possible to create synthetic scrapes, and to keep an existing scrape hot. For best results, avoid leaving any human scent.

I will provide a couple of suggestions. To reduce human scent, always wear rubber boots and use rubber gloves when handling a dispenser and applying scent. Once again, I will stress that big bucks seldom forgive your mistakes. Finally, make certain you avoid brushing against overhanging limbs and surrounding brush.

Synthetic scrapes should be set just before the breeding begins, and in areas a buck will likely travel. However, I don't believe that you should apply scents and attempt to fidget with hot scrapes or scrape lines. I look at it this way: why risk spoiling an ambush opportunity? If a scrape is already active, let the bucks do the job for you, and hope the big one shows.

I can't help but believe that other tactical measures provide the better opportunities, but I will continue to hunt over scrapes when the right opportunity knocks. Scrapes could pay off if your timing is correct, and if you can locate recurring scrapes and scrape lines without interrupting the habits of the super buck you want to kill.

CHAPTER 6

When Big Bucks Become Almost Nocturnal:
How to Beat Them

Each hunting season, many die-hard deer hunters discuss the disappearance of big bucks once the pressure peaks. Most claim that the mature bucks become nocturnal, moving only during the dark hours when they feel most secure.

I won't deny that big bucks disappear shortly after the breeding peaks, and shortly after the hunting intensifies. However, I don't believe that any big buck becomes totally nocturnal and moves only in the dark. They might move less than they did during the rut, and they might move less than they did during the pre-rut era, but it's unlikely that any buck will stay bedded from dawn to dusk. I won't deny that a buck's survival instinct is strong when it comes to taking chances he once did, but the fact remains that he must move and feed. The breeding instinct also sticks with him long after the rut ends, which can also prompt him to move during daylight hours.

With that said, we can suppose that some mature bucks become almost nocturnal. Their daylight movement might be restricted to an hour or so after dawn, and an hour or so before dusk. I also believe that any hunter could ambush a "nocturnal" buck during this brief time if they abandon the once-hot sign that produced action, and look for certain areas that become most attractive to almost-nocturnal bucks.

How the Nocturnal Transition Begins

Before getting into the better ambush locations for pressured bucks, let's first look into the factors that lead to a buck becoming almost nocturnal. In areas with little hunting pressure, a buck might never make this transition. Yet, a hunter who spends ample time in the area could still claim that the big boys have holed up. Keep in mind, all deer retain some nocturnal instincts and have never been completely diurnal. Big bucks do move more in daylight hours during breeding, but hunters should forget the past once the breeding ends.

It's also true that many bucks can't move in daylight hours even if they wanted to. Many don't survive the rut, and no given area is absolutely crawling with large numbers of mature whitetails anyway. Therefore, about the time that some bucks become nocturnal, we can reasonably say there are not as many big bucks to move during the daylight hours.

The firearm season is responsible for bucks becoming near-nocturnal. I don't believe any whitetail is capable of reasoning to the point of knowing that gun season is open and therefore he should head for the hills. However, they are aware of the change in human encroachment. During the firearm season, most areas—public and private—receive far more pressure than during the archery season. It's also true that most firearm seasons are timed for the peak rut when big bucks move most. More hunters are detected by deer, so it's simply a matter of time before all deer adopt the nocturnal habit. You can also assume the mature and educated bucks are the first to notice the changes and adapt accordingly.

In some areas of southern Indiana where I used to hunt every firearm season, I could usually see a change in deer movement

Although deer do not become completely nocturnal, hunting pressure can have a pronounced effect on their movement, restricting much of your ambush opportunities to early and late day.

within a few days of the season opener. After the first few days, the area would dry up and the bucks disappeared. However, like many states, Indiana offers sixteen continuous days of hunting during the firearm season, and shortly thereafter another sixteen days of muzzleloader hunting. Other states provide even more days. While some officials claim that long gun seasons are necessary to control herds, we can't deny that intense hunting affects deer movement.

On the other hand, Illinois offers a three-day gun season during the peak rut and a four-day gun season about ten days later. I've found that the first gun season seldom affects deer movement as seriously as it does in locations where long gun seasons occur. Nevertheless, after the rut begins to subside, the surviving mature bucks still move less in daylight hours and appear to enforce nocturnal instincts.

Ambushing a Nocturnal Buck

Throughout this book, I provide numerous tactics and ideal ambush locations for surprising a huge buck. Most of these ambush methods differ, changing with the season as the habits of bucks and does change—from the pre-rut to peak-rut to late season. I discuss bedding areas a few times, but when it comes to extensive hunting pressure that causes bucks to become nocturnal, the bedding area becomes the hottest ambush location.

The primary reason for hunting a bedding area is simple: the closer you are to where the buck will be in daylight hours, the better the chance you can catch him coming and going. No buck will spend eternity in a bedding area, even if food sources and water are available. He must occasionally leave the security of the bedding area for additional resources. He will also retain a breeding instinct, despite the fact that most mature does have bred. The less distance he must travel to reach you when he leaves the bedding area, the better the chance you will see him during daylight hours.

Consider a buck that you once spotted during the pre-rut period in an agricultural field thirty minutes before dusk. The buck might have traveled several hundred yards to reach you, and might have been moving for more than an hour to get there. Now, consider the same buck with his nocturnal instinct in high gear. He might get up thirty minutes before dusk and browse within the bedding area for another fifteen minutes. If he leaves the bedding area fifteen minutes before dusk, you have no chance of seeing him at the food source, or even along a trail a short distance away from the field. This is how nocturnal bucks earn their name. However, if you are set up close to the bedding area, the possibility exists you could see and even ambush the buck. Perhaps it will be late evening when an opportunity arrives, but as they say, better late than never.

A few years ago, I set up a stand along a fenceline late in the season. The fenceline had become a natural travel zone, and the bedding area that bordered the travel route made it ideal. My tree stand was 50 yards from the bedding area, and nearly as far from the fence. The ambush location couldn't have been better for the short period of firearm season that remained. Shortly before dusk, a huge buck appeared, walking along the fence away from the thick bedding area. Although the nocturnal buck had a broken brow tine, he was an old-timer and carried a heavy-beamed rack with eight points.

Finding a promising bedding area is not always easy. Some areas that once housed a big buck no longer do. As foliage diminishes, so does the attraction of a bedding area. Bucks usually prefer the thickest available cover, and for good reason. This is where they feel the safest.

In Chapter 14, you will read about whitetail sanctuaries and how they attract big bucks. Although the same sanctuary can also attract a nocturnal buck, you must respect it and avoid entering the bedding area. This applies to all bedding areas. It could be a dense pine thicket, or perhaps an area grown up with honeysuckle and briars. The point is, make certain you skirt the perimeters cautiously when scouting for bedding areas and ambush locations. You might get by with pushing an early-season buck out of a bedding area once, or perhaps twice. He might return the next day, or a few days later. However, nocturnal bucks are already on edge. It may well take only one mistake on your part to send him into parts unknown for the remainder of the hunting season.

Although you should avoid entering a possible bedding area, you must scout the perimeter to make sure a deer is there. Trails might not look as impressive near a bedding area as they do in other areas, but they should indicate sign of some wear. Fresh rubs can often be found along the fringe of the bedding area, too. Many big bucks, despite being almost nocturnal, will still leave their marks even though the breeding has ended. Big tracks could also indicate the presence of a super whitetail.

The same big buck is unlikely to use the same bedding area daily. However, I do believe that a safe haven becomes more attractive to a big buck when he needs security most. For one reason, there are fewer bedding areas from which to choose during late fall and early winter. It's also true that a big buck undoubtedly appreciates any area that is providing security at its finest, at a time when he feels the least secure.

While the thickest terrain might provide the best bedding areas for nocturnal bucks, there are other areas you can consider. Excellent choices are those where the least number of hunters have ventured. A remote area might be attractive to a big buck, but it doesn't have to be miles from nowhere.

Consider a waist-high weed field where I set up a stand several years ago. I was hunting with a muzzleloader two weeks after the first firearm season had ended. I saw enough fresh sign along the perimeter of the weed field to attract me, although I remained

Because many mature and educated whitetails move near dusk and dawn, approaching nocturnal behavior, arrive early and leave late to avoid letting a buck know you are there.

skeptical since the area had little to offer in the way of thickets. The weed field was probably less than three acres, and it appeared that a deer could find little in the way of hideouts.

On the second evening, I spotted movement inside the bedding area. My perched position provided a great downward view. My binoculars soon picked out huge bobbing antlers moving perpendicular to my location. I was amazed at how effectively the tall weeds could conceal the big buck, and even more amazed at how quickly he disappeared one minute later. By the way, I never saw that buck again, despite hunting the location at least four times.

Many seemingly unthinkable areas can attract a nocturnal buck. Not long ago, an acquaintance told me about a super buck that suddenly appeared while he was hunting a harvested cornfield one evening. It seems that near one side of the field, there was a 100-yard-diameter circle of standing corn. The hunter happened to be looking at the standing corn when the buck suddenly stood up. The buck was well out of bow range, and the hunter wondered how lucky he was to reach his stand without being spotted by the buck. He also realized how a nocturnal buck would take advantage of anything that provides cover.

People often avoid swampy areas during the hunting seasons. These areas often attract nocturnal bucks, simply because they have been avoided and left undisturbed. While hunting the Muscatatuck National Wildlife Refuge in southern Indiana, I have seen a few hunters leave the area with big bucks. Those bucks didn't mind doing a little wading through some water to reach the best hideouts.

There is one golden rule for hunting nocturnal bucks near bedding areas: arrive early and leave late. I've mentioned that previously in this book, but it's absolutely necessary to adhere to this when bucks do most of their moving during the dark hours. The earlier you get to your ambush location in the mornings, the better the chance you won't push a buck out when you arrive. In the evenings, I would suggest you give it to the last moment of legal shooting time, and stay on stand until darkness prevails.

Even when big bucks appear to be nocturnal, I continue hunting when opportunity allows and a tag is available. I must say, though, that the evenings have provided me with the best hunting. I've seen far more educated whitetails at dusk than I have at dawn, though I hunt some of the same locations near the same bedding areas morning and evening. This leads me to believe that some big bucks might prefer to reach the safety of their hideout before the pink sky appears at first light. That's not to say that morning hunting won't pay off, however. During the rut, I believe mornings provide the best ambush opportunities. When the breeding subsides and the bucks feel pressured, though, evenings seem to produce the most action for me.

It is fortunate that we don't have to hunt nocturnal bucks throughout the archery and gun seasons. The period of nocturnal bucks is brief. Although hunting pressure compels most bucks to become somewhat nocturnal, it can change quickly. Once the hunting pressure subsides, it often takes only a short cooling period before the bucks start moving more often during daylight hours.

CHAPTER 7

Hunting the Barometer:
Respond to Weather Like a Big Buck

C onditions couldn't have been less favorable that after-noon. A cold, brisk wind coupled with light drizzle had dampened my body and spirits. To make matters worse, it was a few days into Indiana's lengthy firearm season, and the bucks had seemingly disappeared. So, with ninety minutes of daylight remaining, I was totally shocked when I spotted the buck moving through the wooded draw.

Although the buck did not carry the headgear for which I had waited, he was the first of three to show up that evening. I caught a glimpse of yet another buck only twenty minutes later. Just before dark, the last one appeared and walked right under my tree. Unfortunately, none of the bucks had made it to their second birthday.

Why was it these bucks moved so readily on a nasty day? At that time, I was unaware that a falling barometer had anything to do with this unusual and exciting activity. In fact, it was the following year, when a similar occurrence took place, that I realized how weather affects buck movement. On another dreadful evening when conditions were miserable, I spotted a buck moving through a thicket. A short distance away, my dad was zeroing in on a huge buck in pursuit of a doe. When his slugster roared, I flinched and a huge nine-pointer dropped.

Upon returning home that night, somewhat exhausted after dragging the buck to the road, I settled in front of the television to catch the weather forecast for the next day. It was then that I heard about a rapidly falling barometer and the approach of a cold front, and it was then that I began to put two and two together. When it might seem to you that a buck would never want to move, that's when he suddenly turns it on.

Effects of a Falling Barometer

These incidents occurred several years ago, and I wasted no time in putting together a magazine story about cold-weather bucks. In the process, somebody suggested that I speak with Dr. Grant Woods, a wildlife research biologist. At that time, he had studied whitetail deer movements for seven years, and demonstrated that deer move considerably more in the daylight hours when the barometer begins to fall rapidly. He also claimed that an increase in movement occurred with the arrival of the first cold front of the season, and that a change of four or five barometric points in a day was very significant.

Although Dr. Woods claimed that overall deer movement was related in part to geography, an increase in movement associated with a falling barometer did not appear to be related to any

Always keep an eye on the weather and figure it into your plans, as deer will typically move about more under certain meteorological conditions, like this buck that exposed itself in reaction to a fast-moving cold front.

specific geographic or climatic region. He collected his data in South Carolina and New York.

To learn the most from my bowhunting experiences, I often keep logs, which show the number of deer seen and harvested from various ambush locations. I also track weather conditions— temperature, humidity, wind direction and speed, and barometer readings. Several years ago I noticed one trend of increased deer movements during approaching weather systems, which became increasingly apparent as I logged the records of ten bowhunters, including myself. We typically saw deer 46 percent of the time on calm days. I'm speaking of the kind of days hunters look forward to being in the woods. However, the most interesting results came when we hunted on windy days, some of which included precipitation, as the barometer began to fall rapidly. On these days, we saw deer an average of 67 percent of our time on stands.

Approaching Cold Fronts

Not long after talking with Dr. Woods, I also discussed falling barometers with a meteorologist. He mentioned that any approaching front usually triggers a drop in barometric pressure. It can fall rapidly, or gently, depending upon strength of the front. The meteorologist also suggested that a cold front will often trigger a rapid decline in the barometer. Warm fronts can cause a drop in the barometric pressure, but seldom a rapid decline. However, once the front begins to stabilize in the area, the barometer begins rising.

From what I have noted, the best buck movement has occurred as the barometer falls, usually just before a cold front arrives. We know that photoperiodism governs the breeding cycle. There's a brief period of a few days when most breeding occurs and when most bucks go wild. Similarly, the falling barometer does temporarily spark buck movement, and this can be before or after the peak rut.

Consider a huge buck I harvested during the 2005 Illinois archery season. We were two weeks away from the peak rut, and the temperature was 68 degrees when I headed out that morning.

Two hours into the hunt, the thermometer started plunging and the wind increased dramatically. I saw three bucks in a short time, including a super ten-pointer with a double brow tine and a very unusual point angling toward his nose. The deer was 70 yards away and about to pass by when I grunted with a high-volume call to get his attention. I shot the deer at 18 yards, attributing my success to the falling barometer that had the bucks moving, and the grunt call that brought him into range.

Timing the Front

I believe timing is crucial when attempting to ambush a mature buck when a front approaches. If you are too early, or too late, you might miss the boat entirely. For instance, if you are on stand two hours before the barometer begins falling, the approaching front probably won't help. Then again, if you reach your ambush location as the barometer begins to stabilize or increase, you could be just a little late.

Just twelve hours before writing this chapter, I climbed into my stand as a cold front approached. Two hours later, I spotted a respectable eight-pointer as he thrashed a tree from side to side. The buck walked by at 25 yards, demonstrating yet another one doing his thing as the barometer fell. The peak rut was several weeks off when this occurred. It was still early in the season when most bucks were only dreaming about what was to come. Yet, this deer was out and about, and feeling his Wheaties as the barometer fell. The event was no surprise, however. I've always found that approaching cold fronts and declining barometers trigger bucks to make more rubs and scrapes.

Who knows what goes through a buck's mind when the barometer crashes? Perhaps he knows that the falling barometer stimulates does to move. We've always known that anytime a weather system (particularly a cold front) approaches, deer move and feed heavily. Also, consider that sometimes heavy rain and/or snow will accompany the front as it crashes with the existing weather system. Deer prefer to feed at the onset of the approaching front and lay up when the heaviest precipitation occurs. From a buck's perspective, he is probably aware that it will be easier for him to locate does.

The food sources might offer the best ambush possibilities, and even the trails provide potential. In fact, I believe that travel corridors should rate near the top. Fencelines, funnels, and other

Snow, rain, wind, pressure changes . . . these can all have an effect on deer behavior, and the smart hunter takes these factors into account.

corridors that connect to the foods are good bets for ambushing a mature whitetail as a front approaches.

Once the barometer begins rising, it appears that you are probably back to normal as far as hunting goes. Dr. Woods stated that one can safely assume that a rising barometer may or may not cause an increase in deer movement. It boils down to how long a system has been stationary. The longer it hangs over a given area, the better deer will move when the barometer begins to rise. Eventually, the barometer will level off, as long as another front is not approaching. Dr. Woods said a steady barometer usually indicates stable weather, unless wind becomes a factor. When a steady barometer is predicted, it might not mean you will see more deer, but you can assume the weather will at least be pleasant for hunting.

I'm not suggesting that bucks move better when the barometer crashes than when the rut peaks. However, the changing barometer is likely to increase buck movement. Moreover, if the rut is close, the results can be dynamite.

This book has no chapter that relates directly to midday hunting. This is a proven tactic whenever the rut is in high gear. I will say, though, that midday hunting can be superb when the barometer falls. I would never suggest you hunt only mornings and afternoons; midday hunting can work effectively just before and during the breeding period. Likewise, a rapid decline in the barometer could cause bucks to move at any hour of the day, regardless of how far off the breeding will occur.

We already know that deer move better on some days than on other days. Of course, deer movement can be affected by hunting pressure, hunger, and various other factors. But many animals, including mature bucks, have a remarkable ability to detect approaching weather systems. They can do this long before we can, if we have not heard a weatherman's forecast. Why else do we often see deer feeding intensely just before a storm arrives?

There are a few ways to keep up with changing weather, including tuning in to radio and television to hear what the meteorologists have to say. We all seem to hold a grudge against the weather-predicting folks, but they often hit it right. You might also consider purchasing an inexpensive portable weather scanner. These devices will let you know exactly what the barometer is doing.

I've never been a fair-weather hunter, but like most, I still look forward to those beautiful, serene days. However, we can almost always count on a falling barometer occasionally during the hunting season. With luck, one or more will occur when you head for the woods. It's not necessarily going to be a comfortable day, but the possibility exists it could be the right day. It only takes the right bad day to make a big buck move that otherwise might have laid up.

CHAPTER 8

Analyzing Antlers:
A Primer in Field-Judging Trophy Whitetails

J udging the size of antlers with some degree of accuracy is an art. Few individuals can do so, even if they have all the time in the world, much less when you have only seconds to determine if a buck is the one you want. I have most certainly made mistakes over the years and on more than one occasion shot a buck that shrank in the time it took me to get to him. But practice makes perfect, and the more you look at antlers, the better you can determine the right buck.

Before proceeding with methods to help you judge antler size, I would like to point out that you should set standards before hunting. Although there are minimum scores for making the record books, you must avoid shooting the wrong buck. Some folks will hunt all their lives and never kill anything better than the typical two-year-old eight-pointer. That's not to say eight-pointers won't surpass trophy status, however. Many do, including a couple of super eights that I've put on the wall. On the other hand, though, most bucks that do make the record books have passed their second birthday. They might or might not carry more than eight points.

You must decide for yourself what you want to shoot, and be prepared to make that decision quickly. If score is most important, this chapter will help you to make an accurate guess at a glance. If it's overall appearance of antlers that matters (which is more often the case with trophy hunters), this chapter will show you ways to identify the right buck without hesitation.

Recognizing Big Antlers When You See Them

I would suggest to anyone that he or she spend time at a local taxidermy studio to familiarize himself with big antlers. There, you often have the chance to compare bucks. For instance, some bucks with eight points and a 15-inch spread look impressive when seen on a wall with no other bucks nearby. These bucks often have Boone & Crockett scores of 105–120 inches, and fall short of the record books. However, if the same mount appears next to a buck scoring 140–150 inches, the difference is unbelievable.

Binoculars are essential for recognizing the right buck in the field. Nonetheless, there are two sides to every story. Binoculars can also cost you when conditions are not favorable. (More about that in a moment.) I prefer three primary features for quick and accurate glassing of a buck: The binoculars must be somewhat compact, offer a wide field of view, and provide glassing opportunities in low light.

I carry small binoculars that can be worn around my neck and tucked into a jacket. They don't interfere with shooting a bow, and they provide quick and easy access. My preferred power and objective lens diameter is 8x42mm. This won't be as compact as an 8x32mm or 8x25mm, but it will provide a wide field of view and allow me to quickly pick up the buck's antlers in low light. Time is of the essence when a buck is approaching, or about to pass by.

When you can watch a buck in a field for a long period, binoculars and/or spotting scopes will provide you with an opportunity to determine antler size exactly. If time allows, you could even take mind measurements and calculate later. This is seldom the case, though, when you wait in ambush and see a buck cross briefly through an open area or walk past you in cover.

Binoculars are sometimes essential for judging a buck's antlers. But when you have only seconds to determine the size of the buck, your eyes might be quicker than your reach.

In most hunting situations, binoculars are beneficial if time allows you to use them before the buck disappears. I have often attempted to use binoculars, only to let a buck get past me, at least far enough that shooting became impossible after recognizing him as the right buck. For this reason, I will rely on my eyes and avoid reaching for binoculars when conditions are unfavorable.

First Impression

When a buck passes your ambush hideout, you seldom have long to decide whether to shoot. It's a decision you must make quickly and without hesitation. Hesitation is costly, as I have discovered on many occasions. Should I shoot, or should I wait for a better buck?

Recognizing a big buck as such when you see one should depend upon your first impression. In other words, if you have doubt about shooting, you probably shouldn't. This is not always true, since antlers are sometimes obscured by debris and your first look doesn't give you an accurate picture, but more often than not, it's the first impression that counts. When you first see a buck, something clicks in your mind that tells you "yes," "no," or "hmmmm." If it says "yes," I suggest you forget about antlers and concentrate on the first shooting opportunity. If your mind registers "no" or "maybe," it is probably not the buck for you.

One year before writing this book, I sat in a tree stand near a two-acre dense thicket. I caught movement of a deer just before dusk as it walked out of the bedding area. As soon as I spotted the antlers, I knew he was the right buck. There were no doubts. I reached for my bow and took my eyes off the antlers, hoping for a shooting opportunity. (Things did not work out in the moments that followed, but that's another story.) I knew the moment I saw this mature buck that he carried the headgear I wanted.

Height and Width

There is a golden rule that comes with analyzing antlers: tall and narrow antlers typically score higher than low, wide antlers. Seldom do you see a buck with tall and wide antlers. The reason that tall, narrow racks score better is that there is more to score. Width adds very few inches, whereas several long points add on immensely.

Determining width is probably one of the easiest evaluation methods when a quick glance is all you get. If a buck faces into you or away, you can estimate width accurately. Consider that the ears of an adult whitetail buck are about 15 inches apart from tip to tip. If the antlers appear to be ear-to-ear, the buck has a spread of about 15 inches. If antlers seem to stick out past the ears, all you need to do is estimate the distance past each ear. Most bucks with a spread of 18 inches or more look most impressive. If you see antlers a couple of inches past each ear, you can assume a buck has a spread of about 19 inches.

However, even a buck with a spread of only 15 inches could look huge if he has tall antlers. And, make no mistake, many bucks with narrow spreads do make it into the record books. One of my best has a spread of only 15.5 inches, but looks far better than a couple of others that are near 20 inches wide. When it comes to antler development, it seems to go one way or the other. If a buck is wide, he isn't likely to have tall points. The less space there is between the antlers, the more likely a mature buck will develop tall antlers.

Although length of points is seldom easy to determine, hunters can usually discern tall antlers as those with points at least eight inches long. Some huge bucks will carry G-2 and G-3 points that surpass 11 inches. The G-2 and G-3 points are the first two points scored past the brow tine, and usually provide the best height of all points.

Number of Points

The total number of points is often discussed amongst hunters. Typical antlers carry eight to twelve points. On rare occasions, some bucks sport numerous points, and there's no doubt that the more points, the more impressive the antlers appear. It's also true that more points mean more inches. However, I'm not so sure that the number of points should play a big role in what you shoot. If a buck carries eight or more, he could be a super whitetail. As mentioned previously, many eight-pointers have enough height to fall into the "trophy" category.

Determining the total number of points is easiest when a buck is broadside. But instead of attempting to count every point, focus on only one antler—that which you can see the best. You need only count the number of points you see coming off the middle of the antler. This is the G-2, G-3, and perhaps a G-4 or G-5, etc. For instance, if you see two points sticking up, the G-2 and G-3, you can safely assume the buck is an eight-pointer. The buck's brow tine and end of the main beam tell you he carries four points on the antler. If the buck also carries four points on the opposite antler, he has eight points. It's a straightforward method that allows you to determine total points at a quick glance. You count the total points you see coming off the main beam, and then add two. Double these totals for both antlers, and you have the total number of points. There are always exceptions, and you could end up with a seven-pointer instead of an eight. On the other

If you see two points up in the middle, the buck is probably an 8-pointer. It's faster to count only points coming off the main beam, and then add two for the brow tine and end of main beam.

hand, you could think you are shooting a buck with eight points and end up with a nine-pointer.

Sleeper Bucks

There are three scoring areas of antlers that are difficult to estimate, yet they are often the most rewarding when a buck's final tally is completed. They are brow tines, length of main beams, and mass. All can add several inches to the score and make a buck appear most impressive.

Brow tines are not easily noticed unless a buck is close, or time allows you to examine him for a long period. However, brow tines can mean several inches, and extra brow tines can really boost the score. Double-brows are uncommon, particularly on both antlers, but long single brow tines that surpass five inches are a big plus when the total score is calculated.

Most big bucks don't have long brow tines. Two or three inches are common, although the remaining portion of the antlers could be large. Yet there are bucks killed every season that have brow tines four to six inches long, and sometimes better. Consider that a buck with two-inch brow tines adds four inches to the score. Now consider a buck with six-inch brow tines. He adds 12 inches to the score—three times more. I don't suggest you look for long brow tines unless opportunity allows. It is something to hope for, though, when a buck is down. Mass and long beam length are additional pluses.

You can judge main beam length by comparing the length of the beam to the deer's head. If a buck is broadside, take notice of how close the antler is to the deer's nose. An antler that is close to the deer's nose is probably 22 or more inches. Some main beams are even longer, but this is rare and I would suggest that you don't wait for a buck with a beam as long as the nose. Most trophy whitetails carry main beams only 18 to 20 inches long. If you see a main beam that extends one-half to two-thirds of the way to the nose, the buck carries a beam of respectable length. You can assume the other beam will be similar to the one you observed.

The only exception to comparing the antler to the head is when the main beam grows upwards. Some bucks have long main beams that do not extend more than halfway to the nose. Instead of a near-horizontal antler beam, it appears slightly vertical. This is not usually the case, but these bucks do exist. They are difficult to judge, and usually appear as likely trophies simply because their height looks impressive.

Because scorers measure circumference of the antler in four locations, mass adds considerably to the score. Determining mass is never easy, however. You might have plenty of time to glass a buck and never tell for sure that he has great mass. When you do look for mass, concentrate on the base of the antlers near the brow tines. If it appears massive at this point, it probably also has mass at other locations where circumference is determined.

Mass is more easily estimated when bucks carry white antlers. They show up much better than dark, walnut-colored antlers. The amount of rubbing, and types of trees rubbed, often play a role in the color of antlers, as do genetics. Mass has nothing to do with the color of a buck's antlers. Hunters do usually notice spindly antlers, and bucks that appear to have thin points seldom have noteworthy mass on the main beams.

This book is not about shooting only the biggest buck roaming the woods. It is about shooting a trophy whitetail. It's irrelevant what your buddy shoots, or whether you shoot one that's bigger than his or hers. It's about recognizing a big one when you see him at quick glance, and knowing he's the right one when you release an arrow or pull a trigger. That is what makes you a trophy hunter.

When I made the decision several years ago to pursue only trophy whitetails, I vowed to shoot only those I would mount: mature bucks and those that appear to be at least three-and-a-half years old. Since then, big antlers have played havoc on my mind, and like other hunters, I have become obsessed with pursuing only those that are trophy caliber. In short, that is usually a buck that surpasses minimum score for the record book.

I would suggest you avoid staring at antlers, trying to count points, etc., when a buck reaches the point of no return. Well-known bowhunter Myles Keller, who has taken numerous Pope-and-Young-caliber bucks, once told me that as soon as he realizes it's the right buck, he takes his eyes off the antlers and concentrates only on the body, waiting for the perfect shooting opportunity.

This advice has assisted me on many occasions. When I first see a big one coming, I make an immediate decision to shoot or not to shoot. If my response is to shoot, I avoid looking directly at the antlers. Antlers are distracting, and they can turn your muscles into jelly. You also must forget about body size. Big-bodied deer look impressive, but it hardly places them in the trophy category. Antlers, and only antlers, count.

Coping with the Fever

Buck fever has been talked about for years. Research has shown that hunters who volunteered to be tested had significant and increased heart rates when any deer suddenly appeared, and much more so when a buck with huge antlers appeared. Has this subject been overemphasized? I don't think so. Unsteady nerves have probably been responsible for more blown opportunities than anything else has.

So, what could happen if buck fever sets in and your heart rate suddenly goes bananas? I won't attempt to get into the medical aspect of what it could lead to, but I will tell you that it could cost you the buck of a lifetime. Hunters have attested to all kinds of problems when a big buck appears. Temporary blindness is one. Some hunters have claimed that buck fever has caused blurred vision to the point of not being able to see the approaching buck. Shakes and rapid breathing, probably the most common symptoms, are also apparent. You could compare buck fever to stage fright!

I also have found it helpful to tell myself that the super buck approaching is not the buck I want. In other words, as the buck comes to me, I convince myself that he's not big enough (although I know better). Meanwhile, I draw the bowstring or shoulder the firearm, aim, and you know the rest of the story. This is a personal coping option, but it has provided me with enough calmness to get the job done.

I've also discovered that the longer it takes a buck to get to you, the more nervous you become. I have been far more effective when I see a buck that is only seconds away from walking into shooting range. If he is far when I first see him approaching, more than likely my nerves will be tested before the shooting opportunity presents itself.

Perhaps the most important factor of this chapter is making sure you are happy when the deer is down. It's easy to err and shoot the wrong buck. I've done it, and so have many others dedicated to tagging a super deer. The better you are at judging a buck, the better the chance you will shoot the right buck.

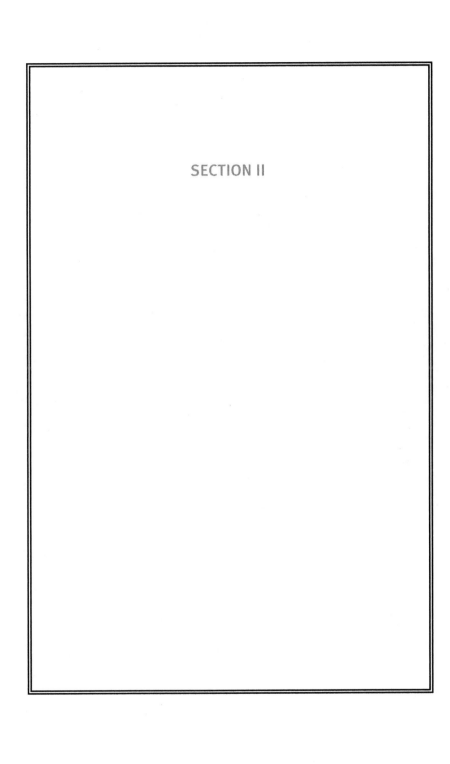

SECTION II

CHAPTER 9

Stay on the Move: *The Multi-Stand System for Big Bucks*

Tree-stand hunting is the most popular method of ambushing deer for archery and gunners, and for good reason: it's the most effective way to surprise any deer, and positively the most desirable technique to beat the odds against tagging a super whitetail. That is, if you stay on the move and apply the multi-stand ambush.

First, let me clarify the "stay on the move" approach. This isn't about moving around within your hunting area at prime hunting time. This is about being in one stand one day and in another the next, and not overhunting any one ambush site.

Why Multiple Stands?

Multiple tree-stand locations allow you to stay on the move, and it makes certain a buck doesn't know where you are, or where you will soon be. In fact, keeping the bucks guessing is the primary reason for using the multi-stand approach. This approach also enables you to hunt where the wind is always favorable. Outdoor writer and wildlife photographer Leonard Lee Rue III once said, "The more photos you shoot, the more you have to choose from." In the case of multiple stands, the more ambush locations you have, the more choices there are.

Consider that you can't get to and from your ambush site without creating disturbance. Climbing in and out, walking in and out, or just sitting there enjoying your surroundings is risky business. Of course, you have to do it to hunt big bucks. The more precautions you take doing it, though, the better the chance you will keep a buck guessing. Using different stands consistently, and seldom hunting the same stand, is the best way to get the task done. As I've said before, big bucks don't make a habit of forgiving your mistakes. It's not always where you are that counts when you wait on a big buck to come in. Oftentimes it's where you've been that could decide whether he will ever show.

I've often heard hunters say that if you see a big buck once and don't get him, you can forget about a second opportunity. There's plenty of truth to this theory, but it's not carved in stone. Home range size and hunting pressure can greatly affect your chances of seeing a big buck more than once. There are many times that I saw a particular buck only once. On other occasions, I've seen the same big buck numerous times. I can still remember one I called "Brownie," so named because of the walnut rack he carried. I saw Brownie at least four times during the archery season. Unfortunately, I never saw him after the firearm season (I assume Brownie bit the big one).

But I managed to see this buck multiple times that season, due to the multi-stand approach I used. I had several stands placed within a half-mile-radius area, and always hunted somewhere

The multi-stand system is one of the best overall approaches for maximizing your chances of drawing on that bruiser buck.

different. I was able to keep Brownie guessing and, as far as I know, the buck never knew he was being hunted.

Playing the wind correctly is essential to all successful deer hunting, and applies no less in multi-stand scenarios. Most deer hunters don't want to hear about hunting where the wind is favorable, primarily because we've heard it too many times. Nevertheless, I suspect more big bucks are saved by wind each season than for any other reason. I set up stands to compensate for wind direction long before I actually hunt the site. In other words, I want to make sure I can choose a stand that is favorable regardless of wind direction. I even set up a stand for the peculiar easterly wind. An easterly is rare, but it happens occasionally through the hunting season.

Number of Ambush Sites

When hunting near home, I typically hang about a dozen portable tree stands each season, then move several throughout the remainder of the season. It's hard work, but it's worth the effort. I've always believed I have to hang so many stands, walk so many miles, miss so much sleep, etc., before I'm allowed a shooting opportunity. That's a crazy philosophy, I know, but I also believe that the harder I work, the luckier I get.

It might or might not be feasible for you to find numerous ambush sites. The size of your hunting area might affect the number of sites, as does hunting pressure. However, you can ensure an effective multi-stand tactic if you can select four or five ambush locations.

Keep in mind, you don't have to spread your ambush sites over miles of country in different hunting areas. Each season, I have stands no more than 100 yards apart. Some are a little farther apart. Some are considerably farther apart. The point is, you should avoid clinging to only one or two stands throughout the hunting season.

Although any type of quality stand has what it takes to help you harvest a super whitetail, there are pros and cons to owning fixed-position, ladder, and climbing stands. You must decide this for yourself. Comfort, expense, ease of setup, etc., will affect your decisions. However, I suggest you keep the disturbance factor in mind. The more difficult it is to set up or use a particular stand, the better the chance a big buck will discover you are there before you hunt.

Climbing stands are extremely popular, and they offer versatility in that you can move a few yards here and there, hunting where wind is favorable. But when you set up several hang-on stands, they are always there and ready for you. I also believe that fixed-position portables do a better job of keeping my presence unknown in a big buck's territory. I don't have to pack in anything except essentials when I hunt, nor will I create much, if any, disturbance getting into the stand.

Burning It Up

It's difficult to avoid hunting the best location repeatedly. It's human nature to repeatedly visit the site where you recently spotted a super whitetail, or perhaps the site that provides the foremost sign. However, I seldom hunt the same stand twice in a row.

Keep in mind, most ambush sites provide the best activity the first two or three times they are hunted. The first time is often the very best. I can't tell you the number of times I've harvested, or came close to tagging, a mature whitetail the first time I used a particular tree-stand site. After reading this far in this chapter, I'm sure you can understand why the first time or two offers the best opportunity to tag a mature buck.

After hunting a site numerous times, activity typically drops off. That's why it's necessary to hunt fresh locations, or at least allow one to cool down before returning. You can get by with hunting one site numerous times, providing you visit the ambush location no more than every few days. This way, each time you are at the site it's almost like you're hunting it for the first time.

Ideal Multi-Stand Setups

Throughout this book, we discuss hot ambush locations for fooling big bucks. We've also talked about the rut—how it compares to pre-rut and post-rut periods when bucks stick to home ranges. Thus, you might assume that during the breeding time, when big bucks move consistently in search of does, using the multi-stand approach might not be as important. While that theory could apply, you must remember that during the rut you must also keep the does guessing. In fact, mature does can play havoc with your chances of intercepting a mature buck. If the does aren't there during the rut, you can forget about seeing big bucks.

With this in mind, I suggest that you apply the same principles throughout the hunting season when choosing ambush sites. There are plenty of folks who hunt with both bow and gun. Some of these individuals change tree-stand-hunting tactics as necessary to accommodate the weapon they use. In other words, if they can shoot far, they make sure they can see farther and so place a stand in an open area. However, that's a mistake that can cost you.

First, consider that bucks like thick cover. I look at it this way—I'd rather see fewer deer and be where the best buck is likely to appear, than to see more deer and have little chance of the big one being there. Don't get me wrong; I love seeing deer. Sometimes it's necessary to keep me going. However, I avoid setting up multiple stands in areas where you can see forever, just to shoot to the maximum range of the gun. There are always exceptions—such as hunting along fringes of fields, powerlines, and areas where you might cover a ridge—but if it comes down to choosing the open hardwoods or the thickets, I'll typically be where I can see the least.

Tree selection is vital. Ambushing mature bucks sometimes means making certain the does and insubordinate bucks get past you first. Whenever I select trees for stand placement, I choose those with the best cover. During the pre-rut when foliage is thicker, you'll have an easier time finding a tree with limbs that provide foliage and background cover, but that time is short-lived. If you hunt often, you'll want to select trees that provide cover even after the foliage diminishes.

I love clumps of trees. Those with three or four main trunks, or simply several other trees close by, provide much-needed cover and increase my chances of avoiding detection when shouldering a gun or drawing my bow. Numerous nearby trees also provide ideal hanging slots for accessories or your weapon, keeping you organized at the moment of truth.

Clearing shooting lanes is usually necessary, particularly for bowhunters, but clearing too much can severely compromise your ambush location. Consider a huge buck that approached my tree stand, back in the late 1980s, in what seemed to be a no-miss opportunity. He was on a steady walk toward me and, had he stayed on course, would have surely passed within 15 yards of my stand, easy bow range. That changed less than a dozen rapid heartbeats later, however. The buck stopped at thirty paces and gazed at the cleared area surrounding my tree. Then he turned and casually walked back the way he came.

I've never forgotten that buck, although the incident occurred almost twenty years ago. Nor have I forgotten how I had cleared too much. That lesson came at the expense of a big buck, but it has certainly helped me since to remain conscious of clearing, and to tag other whitetails.

All deer know their surroundings well. They know exactly how the area is supposed to look, and they will not accept a change to the area until they become used to something new. A buck on the move and in strange territory during the peak rut might not be alarmed upon a major area change, but before and after the rut every buck knows his home range the way you know your backyard.

The sooner you clear an area, the more time a buck has to get used to the new surroundings. This isn't always possible, as we often choose locations at the spur of the moment. Nonetheless, if time allows and you know you will be hunting a certain location, do your clearing long before the hunting begins.

In fact, I hang many portable stands in late summer and early autumn. This gives the area time to "cool down." I might move or place stands during the hunting season after discovering a reason to do so, but some tried-and-true areas should be given immediate attention before the season begins.

Sites That Pay Off Consistently

We've all heard the old saying, "Some got it, and some don't." This theory applies to ambush sites as well as to everyday life.

Yes, there are stand sites that consistently pay off—those you can count on year after year to produce big-buck action. However, I believe these sites are extremely rare. Some hunters, after tagging a super whitetail, can't let go of a certain ambush location and rely on it each season. I, too, have become dependent on several ambush locations, but most of these are proven sites for attracting all deer and only an occasional mature buck. Few stand sites attract whopper bucks on a regular basis.

Since the late 1960s, when I actually began using tree stands (some of these were permanent stands), I've come across only two that I can honestly say were no-fail sites. One was located smack-dab in the middle of a 40-acre thicket. I tagged a buck there each year for eight consecutive seasons, including several good ones. It also provided my son with action. The stand was situated along a trail that bordered a sanctuary that we never penetrated. Visibility was poor, but you could usually count on any buck you spotted to walk by within effective shooting range. Unfortunately, the area died once a portion of the land was cleared for farming.

In the 1990s, I faithfully hunted one area for a number of years. This was on leased land, and although hunting pressure was extreme, it produced two super whitetails and numerous other sightings of big bucks. I always placed my stand along a hillside and a secondary trail. I never really understood why big bucks loved traveling this route more than others nearby, but I soon learned that I could depend on the area season after season.

Looking back, the similarities of these locations were few. The only thing they had in common was dense cover. Food sources were not a factor, nor did the rut play a key role. Bucks used both areas during the pre-rut period as well as the breeding period. Obviously, though, both areas attracted mature bucks.

Although I'm still hoping to come across another dependable site someday, I don't spend my hunting season thinking about finding one, nor do I stick with one site for years thinking it is surely the best place to be. You have to make the ambush possible, and you'll probably kill far more super bucks if you believe they won't always come to the same ambush location.

Nevertheless, I won't deny that knowing every crack and cranny of your area can make some difference when it comes to choosing multiple ambush sites. The more you learn and hunt your area, the more you will come to know where bucks travel and spend their time. Some areas, however, do attract bucks year after year. There are reasons why they do, and you will certainly help your future ambush strategies if you learn why these locations consistently become a magnet for big bucks. Perhaps a certain dense thicket and its inherent security brings in the big ones. Who knows? And while these sites should always be included in your multiple-stand approach, I would not suggest you rely on them for hunting day after day.

Hunters using the ambush method kill most trophy whitetails, and most hunters harvest whitetails using tree stands. It's been that way since we began pursuing white-tailed deer, and rest assured that the multi-stand approach will remain the most deadly tactic for ambushing trophy bucks for years to come.

Consider the 2003 Readership Study conducted by F+W Publications, publishers of *Deer & Deer Hunting Magazine*. It indicated that 92.6 percent of respondents hunted from an elevated stand, and that 39 percent of all deer hunters had purchased a tree stand during the twelve months preceding the study. Absent from the study, though, is the number of hunters that rely upon using multiple stands. I believe that very few hunters do, although it is an absolutely necessary tactic for consistently fooling big bucks.

Discreetness is, perhaps, the most important factor in making your multi-stand ambush strategies work. You can spend a lot of time finding a location that looks best for intercepting a huge buck, but you should never rely on only that one location to make it happen.

CHAPTER 10

The Eye-to-Eye Ambush:
Taking a Trophy on the Ground

Although the previous chapter emphasized the importance of using numerous tree stands to ambush a super buck, many hunters often bypass great ambush locations if trees are absent, or if they do not have an available tree stand. In fact, a ground ambush location with bow or gun could be part of the multi-stand tactic. Hunting on the ground is another ambush choice that will keep the bucks guessing, and it provides another choice that prevents hunting only one tree stand site. Granted, success on the ground is tougher to accomplish, but there are excellent opportunities for those who accept the risk.

Hot Ground-Ambush Sites

Within your hunting range, you might locate thickets surrounded only by saplings and small trees. Big trees aren't the only way to keep a mature buck happy. A dense thicket provides a great ambush opportunity if you can play your cards right.

Visibility could very well play the primary role in the effectiveness of your ground ambush location. I've always believed that the better you can see, the better the chance it won't work, something to which I have alluded in the previous chapter. Always assume this theory, regardless of whether you hunt with bow or gun, from a tree, or on the ground.

Naturally, you must consider your effective shooting range when deciding where to set up in relation to the location of trails, rub lines, and food sources. I believe that closer is better. In other words, when hunting with a bow I often select ground ambush

Although most successful hunters prefer tree stands to ground sites, the fact remains that a number of excellent deer are successfully ambushed in this manner every season.

sites within 20–30 yards of where I expect a big buck to show. This is my effective shooting range. However, even when hunting with a gun, I might set up a little further from where I hope the big buck will show, but I don't make it a point to be 100 yards from where I expect deer to be. Then I rely mostly on the ambush site to make sure I remain hidden and can move as necessary to shoulder a gun or draw the bow.

I seldom attempt ground hunting in open hardwoods or along the fringes of fields. Although a certain wooded or agricultural area can be a hot spot, these areas probably won't provide sufficient cover to keep you hidden. Thus, I apply ground-hunting tactics where dense cover exists, and to cover an area that has not previously been hunted, when a tree stand is not an option.

Many times, as you discover new areas while scouting during the season, you come across one that looks appealing. When you hunt on the ground, you won't have to disturb the area as much as when packing in and setting up a stand. It might require a little work to get it ready, but you can take precautions to keep the location hot.

Natural Foliage or Blind?

In recent years, we've seen a number of new ground blinds introduced by manufacturers. The construction of these nifty outfits will keep you hidden and allow body movement, but I'm not so sure commercial camouflage blinds are your best choice for hunting big bucks on the ground. If you can set up a blind in advance of your hunt, to allow deer to get used to the new object, then you might enjoy positive results. Nevertheless, all deer quickly notice even a small blind set up in an area where it has never been before. Additionally, they aren't likely to walk by it haphazardly. And if you alert the does, you can positively count on a big buck to avoid your ground ambush location.

I typically use natural foliage and debris in which to hide, without piling it too much around me. Too much construction creates disturbance, and it could end up looking as obvious as the manufactured blind. The natural cover is always there, and every big buck in the area won't necessarily want to stare a hole into it if and when he shows. Instead, he is likely to move past the natural stuff without suspicion.

I consistently use logjams, typically clusters of fallen timber, in which I can nestle down and keep most of my body hidden. These are found almost everywhere, and they allow you to move your lower extremities without being detected. Equally important, you don't have to worry about a background.

When downed timber is not readily available, I select the thickest natural foliage to use. Honeysuckle thickets are ideal ambush locations, as is other dense vegetation. The key is to have as much or more cover behind you than in front of you. You must blend with your surroundings and make certain you are not silhouetted.

Pruning shears are necessary when using natural foliage. Oftentimes you must clip debris and place it around you, or use the shears to open a couple of shooting lanes. Make certain you can draw your bow or shoulder a gun without bumping into debris. That may seem basic, but you'll be surprised how it can cost you if you don't test your ambush location before the buck of your dreams appears.

Because ground stands have inherent drawbacks to them, you must maximize whatever you can about the one you do use. Here, the author clears away obstacles to clear shooting lanes.

A few years ago, I set up in a briar thicket to cover a rub line during the pre-rut period. I cleared a couple of shooting lanes in front of me, and made it a point to draw my bow a couple of times to make certain no debris was in the way. One hour later, a huge buck appeared to my left side. With the buck only 15 yards away and his head turned and looking away, I drew my bow. Unfortunately, I had to rise to clear a stem of briars. That worked, but then I spotted additional debris between the buck and me. I picked what I thought was a workable opening, but that failed—upon releasing the arrow, it struck debris immediately upon leaving the bow. It stuck into the ground just short of the buck.

An arrow hitting a limb or debris is the oldest excuse in the book, but can easily happen when hunting on the ground. Needless to say, imagine how I felt after selecting the right ambush location that led to a 160-inch buck walking into easy shooting range, only to see him run off unscathed.

The Comfort Factor

Sitting provides the most comfort. It keeps you from moving, and often keeps you better hidden. I typically carry a small fold-up stool for ground hunting. It is inconspicuous, and fits well in tight places. A small seat with adjustable legs is ideal, allowing you to adjust your height accordingly to the debris around you. Some manufacturers also offer seats with legs that can adjust to uneven or sloped terrain. Many times I've found myself sitting along a hillside, and it doesn't take a 45-degree angle to make a fixed seat uncomfortable. The slightest incline can have you leaning downhill, and ready to move five minutes after you arrive.

When standing is necessary, as it sometimes will be, select a clump of trees in which you can station yourself. This gives you something to lean on, and the trunks of the trees will provide cover.

In an upcoming chapter, you'll read about one of my best bucks taken on the ground with bow and arrow. I was hunting from a ground ambush site, and standing between a clump of three maple trees. There are plenty of reasons why the site paid off, but I mention it now to let you know that ground hunting does work if you can remain hidden.

Each season, I will hunt at a few ground ambush locations— sometimes with a bow, and sometimes with a gun. I love rattling antlers from ground locations, and believe rattling is far more effective on the ground than from a tree. However, most of all I select a ground blind when I must hunt a new spot and to provide another option to ambush a big buck. Trees might be handy, but if time doesn't allow me to set up a stand, I would rather hunt on the ground than select one of my tree stands that offers less promise. Invariably, I've enjoyed plenty of action on the ground, and believe it can provide an exciting element of surprise that many trophy hunters overlook.

The author's best bow-killed buck, taken on the ground in the last seconds of daylight. A well-done sequence of rattling did the trick. The buck scored almost 160 inches (see Chapter 14).

The author's son, John Trout III, took this 10-pointer after several years of waiting for the right customer. Passing smaller bucks is never easy, but it's the only way you will get an opportunity at the right one.

Indiana hunter Scott Ricer took this Boone & Crockett–class buck in the 1990s, the result of lots of dedication and many hours in the woods using the advanced tactics discussed in this book.

Indiana hunter Dean Stallion with a 189-inch buck that he took during the rut, after making a bet that the buck would use a secondary trail.

One of two fabulous bucks the author took by staking out a big oak tree (see Chapter 13). This buck gross scored 141 2/8.

This 145-inch buck was the second the author took at his oak-tree ambush site two days after arrowing the deer on the previous page (see Chapter 13).

The author's wife, Vikki Trout, checks out a large rub. While big and small bucks might rub any size tree, substantial damage like this is made by a buck with serious headgear.

The author staked out a trail near a bedding area during the rut to take this big whitetail, having observed the buck two other times during the late pre-rut of the archery season (he shot the buck on the opening day of the firearm season). Bedding areas provide plenty of opportunity for an ambush several hours after dawn.

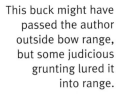

This buck might have passed the author outside bow range, but some judicious grunting lured it into range.

Busted! This buck looked right at the author and bolted seconds later. Lesson: Don't push hard or too far into sanctuaries.

A combination of pre-rut behavior, blowing wind with an approaching cold front, and effective grunting put the author on an intercepting course with this 2005 Illinois prize.

John Trout III took this Indiana 10-pointer several years ago just after dawn on the opening day of the firearms season.

Patterning does led to these two rutted-up bucks that, rather than being interested in fighting, are trying to scent the same thing: does.

This big-bodied, wide-racked monster buck turned up after the author set up an ambush site at a promising scrape line along a field.

Indiana hunter Mark Williams took this 154-inch buck during the peak breeding cycle. During the rut, you can reduce your focus on rubs and scrapes and plan your ambush sites where you find the does.

CHAPTER 11

The Sanctuary:
Secretive Micro-Habitats of Big Bucks

Not long before writing this chapter, I completed a magazine story about constructing whitetail sanctuaries. Few hunters have the means of making their own sanctuary, but almost every hunting area has a sanctuary that mature bucks see as a haven. This chapter will help you to recognize such an area, and to locate good ambush locations nearby.

In laymen's terms, a haven is a refuge or shelter. A whitetail haven is indeed a place that a deer seeks refuge and is typically an area largely undisturbed by human encroachment. A dense grove, small or large, consisting of various types of vegetation that can hide a super buck and allow him to feel secure, is the ultimate sanctuary. However, don't confuse a sanctuary with deer yards. Deer do yard up in some northern regions when temperatures plummet and snow accumulates. The haven I speak of is made up of thick hideouts that attract super bucks any time during the hunting season.

I sincerely believe that no other ambush tactic surpasses the discovery of the right haven. Setting up near a sanctuary is not a seasonal tactic like others previously discussed in this book; it is capable of producing a trophy whitetail during any portion of the hunting season. It can provide payoffs during the pre-rut period when big bucks are more interested in hiding than in does. It can produce results during the peak rut, simply because the does will also hide out in the refuge. During the post-rut era, after the bucks have become educated, the haven will attract mature bucks consistently as they become increasingly nocturnal.

And there's more good news. Sanctuaries typically provide an abundance of food. Although the thick undergrowth of a haven offers nutrition and necessary food during the winter months, it will also supplement deer during early autumn.

The sanctuary also takes a little guessing out of the hunt. When setting up along rubs, scrapes, trails, and foods, there are many more obstacles for the trophy hunter. For instance, wind direction often eliminates some locations' usability for several days. But when hunting a haven, you can often set up along the side of the dense area where the wind is favorable, thereby avoiding the side where the wind blows your scent into the refuge.

The Sanctuary Ambush

Just how dependable is a sanctuary? Consider that a haven is a bedding zone. If it is located in the right area and the hunter remains cautious, a haven will produce far more results than buck signposts, typical trails, and food sources. The hunter who sets up nearby has a much better opportunity of ambushing a super buck later in the mornings and earlier in the evenings. Consider a buck that heads for the sanctuary thirty minutes before dawn. If you are set up along a trail some distance away from the haven, the buck might be long gone before you arrive. On the other hand, if you have set up close to the haven, the same buck might be there after dawn and during shooting light.

Several years ago, my son John took his best buck ever while hunting close to a refuge. It was a forty-year-old strip-mined area, overrun with small narrow hills and covered with dense honey-suckle and other vegetation. He shot the massively antlered, 164-inch buck shortly after dawn broke on the opening morning of Indiana's firearm season.

Any thicket within your hunting area can serve as a sanctuary and hide a super buck. It could be a large 15- or 20-acre spot

Sanctuaries mean the same to bucks as they do to humans – a place where one can be, or at least feel, safe. Be prepared to find such spots in areas with thick growth.

nestled in the middle of hardwoods, or it could be a one-acre thicket amongst agricultural fields and woodlots. In John's case, he was set up on the sanctuary's fringe. The old strip-mine area consisted of small, rolling hills laced with Virginia pines and deciduous trees. The hills and cover provided everything the big buck needed to remain secure.

The thicker the area, the more attractive the sanctuary appears to a mature buck. Size can affect your chances of ambushing a big buck near a haven, and despite what you might think, sometimes smaller is better.

I have access to 40 acres of hunting land on which there are three small sanctuaries. The largest is about two acres, and the other two are no more than one acre each. All provide excellent hunting opportunities, primarily because the smaller havens remove some of the guesswork when planning the ambush. The fewer spots a buck will have to enter and leave the sanctuary, the less guesswork you will have.

Large havens of dense foliage will nevertheless attract deer, but it is also more difficult to select the best ambush locations near them. A large area means more hideouts within the haven, and more trails going in and out. Consider one sanctuary I hunted many years ago. The entire area was about 40 acres, but within this haven were about 20 acres of extremely thick brambles and honeysuckle. The bucks loved it, but their travel routes were anywhere and everywhere; sitting in the right location was tricky business.

It's worth comparing this to an area that has funnels, fencelines, and travel corridors in and near farmland. The areas deer choose to travel are those that provide cover, and it's easier to pattern a buck because they have limited travel zones. Large sanctuaries consisting of thickets could leave you guessing, keeping you unable to pinpoint the best travel routes coming and going from the sanctuary. The bucks are much less predictable and will probably use numerous trails, whereas in a small sanctuary the travel routes you find along the sanctuary will be limited.

Fine-Tuning the Ambush

Shape does not govern the quality of havens. Some are square while some are oval. Some are narrow but long. Although I do believe sanctuaries that are similar in size on all sides offer the best ambushing possibilities, don't think for a moment that an oddly shaped refuge won't provide action. It's a matter of where you set up.

First, consider nearby food sources and the purpose of the haven. The haven is the bedding ground, and the nearby food is the attractant. Unlike the traditional approach of setting up halfway between the food source and the bedding area, the sanctuary provides better results when the hunter stays close.

A nearby food source will make any haven better, but that's not to say it should be close to the sanctuary. On the contrary, the ideal situation is a food source 100 to 300 yards from the sanctuary (alias bedding ground), assuming we are talking about crops or another food source in an open area. I have found some thick havens located right against a food source, but these areas seldom produced positive results. And always consider cover—when a buck leaves a sanctuary, he prefers not to pop out in an open arena. A sanctuary that has at least 50 yards of timber, saplings, or other cover between it and the food source is probably the best scenario.

When selecting an ambush location, I prefer to be within 30–50 yards of the sanctuary. I don't like getting closer, primarily because of disturbance. On the other hand, getting too far away can also hurt your chance of intercepting a big buck. The farther away you are, the farther a buck must travel away from the sanctuary to reach you. Moreover, the farther he travels, the better the chance he will change directions before reaching your ambush site.

Near many havens you will find a travel route bordering the area. You could find trails along all sides, but most often you will see them along only portions of the sanctuary. Bucks love to skirt the sanctuary, particularly during the rut, hoping to pick up a doe's scent. These border trails offer excellent hunting opportunities, providing you use caution and create as little disturbance as possible when setting up and hunting the travel route.

Only a few days before this chapter was prepared, Vikki shot a buck that was traveling a trail perpendicular to the sanctuary. It was early autumn, and our stand was located only a short distance from the haven, allowing a perfect bowhunting ambush location. The trail followed the fringe of the refuge for a distance of about 60 yards before fading into the woods not far from a food source. We had also found a fresh scrape along the trail. Rubs and scrapes are very common around the fringes of sanctuaries. For some reason, bucks love to leave signposts when they walk into and out of sanctuaries.

Obvious trails are also found leading to and from the refuge. Some trails are less visible in woods outside the haven but show up distinctly where they hit the thick stuff. I would suggest you find more than one ambush location near a sanctuary, though, just so you have options. You must hunt where the wind is favorable, which of course means never setting up where your scent blows into that patch of prime real estate.

Hunting near sanctuaries in the mornings can be a tricky business. If you set up where the wind blows toward the food source or other routes coming to the haven, you will be scented before the buck arrives. If you set up where your scent blows into the sanctuary and away from where you expect deer to come from, you would likely be scented by any buck that comes into the sanctuary from another location. Thus, when hunting mornings, make certain to avoid both of these. This may be done by seeking a wind blowing along the perimeter of one side, or slightly away from the sanctuary but not toward the trail you hunt.

Because the wind is never entirely favorable when hunting close to a haven in the morning, I usually prefer the afternoon hunt if the wind blows away from the haven. Remember that a big buck takes his sanctuary very seriously, and one goof by the hunter might be all it takes to blow the whistle and spoil it for future hunts.

Avoid Penetrating Sanctuaries

While we're at it, I might as well provide another warning. A hunter should consider a sanctuary a "closed area." It must remain off-limits throughout the hunting season. Never go into an area you suspect could be a haven. Running a big buck out of the area could have devastating results. Big bucks think of their refuge as a safe-guard, and making a surprise visit won't do you any good. It's always tempting to walk into a sanctuary, just to see what you find, but it's necessary to avoid that temptation. Your assessment of the haven's quality should depend upon the sign you find around it and what you see using the area. If you do want to take a look inside the haven, wait for winter after the hunting seasons end. This is a great time for scouting, and offers an opportunity to hunt for sheds.

Although you know your stomping grounds well, and are probably aware of the thickest cover, I would suggest you make it a point to scout the area thoroughly to ensure there is no sanctuary of which you may have been previously unaware. Again, it doesn't take a large area to supply the ingredients of a safe haven. Even many public hunting lands have sanctuaries. Some are natural due to wind damage that has caused blowdowns. Some wildlife management departments often do work on public hunting ground, cutting timber or burning selected areas to allow new growth. You might be surprised how quickly some of these areas become a sanctuary and allow a buck to grow old.

Constructing a Haven

If you own land, or perhaps hunt private land, you might consider making your own whitetail haven. If you hunt private land, you will certainly need to ask permission before attempting to construct a sanctuary.

The three sanctuaries on the 40 acres I mentioned previously were all man-made. It takes only a chainsaw, a pair of safety glasses, and a little knowledge of cutting trees. I've never been fond of removing timber, even a small section, but I do know that many species of wildlife benefit from cutting. Wild turkeys, for example, have used the fringes of my sanctuaries for nesting. At the other end of the spectrum, I also believe that too much timber cutting can be detrimental to wildlife. A diversity of habitat is beneficial. Deer would much rather have a little of each than one or another.

I seldom cut mast timber. I prefer leaving oaks and other trees that provide food. I do remove other timber, such as the sunlight eaters that provide little or no benefit to wildlife. The sanctuaries I constructed were done in one day. Thus, it's not a major job unless you intend to remove large trees. If you do, you should seek a professional.

One need remove only small sections of timber for new growth to start, and you do not have to do supplemental planting. Many types of thorny bramble bushes, honeysuckle, and other vegetation will often flourish during the first summer of growth. A small quantity of existing vegetation before cutting will provide a faster growing season. A summer drought will slow the growth process, while a fertilizer like JR SimPlot Fertilizer Company's 12–12–12 (referring to the respective percentages of nitrogen, phosphate and potash) might enhance growth if applied just before rain. You can apply the fertilizer somewhat evenly with the assistance of a hand-held seeder.

If you do intend to construct a haven, I would suggest you begin the project in late winter before the spring green-up begins. The idea is to have the sunlight coming into the area when the spring rains arrive and the vegetation growth begins. And, in consideration of havens' locations in comparison to those of food sources, there's one last pointer: If there's water within the sanctuary, it's that much better for attracting big bucks. Even a small ditch running through it will help. A buck is sure to take up residence in a location that has everything he needs.

Deer do not prefer timbered areas that are thick with treetops and entanglements. They like to maneuver freely, and will not spend time in an area where they must jump over obstructions to escape. If you construct your own haven, make certain to pile some of the debris to leave travel routes within the refuge.

One other word of caution: avoid being too sanguine about your targeted refuge, attractive as it may be. A sanctuary will attract big bucks, but I don't believe that the same deer will make it

If opportunity allows, consider constructing your own sanctuary. The removal of some trees is all it takes to bring in sunlight and start new growth. In one summer, a clearing could become a preferred bedding area for a super buck.

a point to bed down in the same haven daily. Mature whitetails are often creatures of habit, but don't assume they will rely on only one bedding area.

Although recent chapters have focused on numerous ambush methods to tag a trophy whitetail buck, I must rate sanctuary hunting at the top. Bedding areas provide the best opportunities. Deer are somewhat meticulous about where they hide, and will often crawl into the smallest nook if it's thick. If you have a sound understanding of sanctuaries, you can take advantage of them when the deer do.

CHAPTER 12

Tale of a
Scrape-Line Buck

Indiana's firearm season was a few days away as I headed for the woods to scout and find a suitable ambush location for opening morning. The rut would soon peak, and buck sign was not difficult to locate. I carried a portable stand on my back and a few screw-in steps in my fanny pack, just in case I might find a hot spot that offered promise.

I had walked for nearly an hour when I located a trail along the side of a small ridge. Then I found a scrape. Then another, and another. I continued to walk the scrape line for a short distance, until I could see a dense thicket ahead that I assumed was a bedding area. Slowly, I retraced my steps to look for a suitable ambush site along the scrape line.

There were several trees in the hardwoods that hid the scrape-line trail, but I promptly decided upon hanging the stand in the middle of a clump of white oaks. There was plenty of cover to conceal me, and the site would be no more than 35 yards from the scrape line. Visibility was fair in both directions along the trail, and the stage was set if the right buck would show.

When dawn broke on opening morning, I was already in the stand and sitting comfortably. I planned to stay through midmorning, as the rut had now peaked. That was providing, of course, that a super buck hadn't already traveled the scrape line early in search of a hot doe.

Activity began shortly after dawn. A doe and two fawns ambled through the woods a short distance from the scrape-line trail. They browsed on acorns as they moved closer to the dense thicket at the end of the ridge, but never once visited any of the scrapes.

Minutes after the doe and fawns had vanished, I spotted a deer walking the ridge coming toward me. I was somewhat surprised to see that he was coming from the thickets and the probable bedding area. But then again, that's how it can work during the rut. You never know for certain where a deer will come from.

I did not see antlers, and assumed the approaching deer was a doe. However, as it crossed the 50-yard line, I saw his glistening white rack against the early-morning sun. The one-and-a-half-year-old buck carried six points. He walked the scrape line but never once stopped to work any of them.

The next couple of hours remained dead. Nothing moved. Unseasonably mild temperatures also began to take their toll on me. In fact, I was considering removing my outer jacket when I again spotted movement. However, this deer was doing what I expected, walking the trail along the ridge and heading toward the thickets. I thought I saw antlers as the deer walked through numerous saplings, but had begun to doubt myself. Then he hit an opening along the scrape-line trail about 60 yards away from my ambush location. He carried a heavy-beamed, walnut-colored rack. The dark antlers were difficult to see, and equally hard to judge. However, a few rapid heartbeats later I knew this buck was exactly what I had hoped for. I shot the buck at 30 yards. He kicked out his back legs and went into his final run, piling up 60 yards later.

I stayed put for a few moments, regaining my composure. As always, though, I find this nearly impossible after shooting a super buck, so I climbed down and headed for the trophy white-tail. After a few oohs and aahs, I closely inspected his massive antlers. His greatest qualities were the long main beams and super six-inch brow tines. Unfortunately, the nine-pointer had a broken G-3 on the right antler.

Rubs vs. Scrapes

As you know from reading Chapter 5, I have always put more emphasis on rubs than scrapes. Nevertheless, if a hunter can locate a scrape line, or possibly a recurring scrape that becomes active each year, the possibility exists that he or she can ambush a buck. Timing is important, however.

In the case of the scrape line I located, the breeding was about to peak. Bucks love traveling such a scrape line during the rut, hoping they will also find a hot doe. Granted, it's not always the scrapes that interest the bucks during the rut. They don't necessarily travel scrape lines to work scrapes, or to see if a doe has visited the scrape and left scent. Bucks create scrape lines along the best trails—those that does use consistently, and those that usually lead to bedding areas or secluded foods. A trail with numerous scrapes shows the hunter that it is a trail used by does. We also know that you must hunt the does when the breeding is about to begin. In the case of a scrape line, you are actually hunting the does.

The two bucks I saw that morning were walking the scrape-line trail. They traveled the trail from opposite directions, but their thoughts were the same. Each hoped to find an estrous doe along the trail. Moreover, had I stayed put that morning and not shot the nine-pointer, I sincerely believe I would have seen additional bucks before lunchtime. I also felt that this scrape line was one of the best I had ever located.

When I had scouted the area and walked this trail days earlier, I found only four scrapes. The distance from the first to the last was about 200 yards. There might have been more scrapes, but I called off the scouting endeavor before the trail entered the thickets. The distance between scrapes varied. The first two scrapes were about 30 yards apart, yet 60 yards separated the second and third scrapes.

Recognizing the Scrape Line

Hunters often fail to locate scrape lines because they don't follow the trail far enough to determine that an actual line existed. We often discover a scrape and believe it to be a sporadic scrape that doesn't tie into others. It is true that scrape lines are rarer than sporadic scrapes—you might locate fifty to a hundred scrapes late in the pre-rut period within a square mile, yet there could be fewer than one or two scrape lines.

If you do locate a scrape line, I would not necessarily attempt to determine whether or not big buck sign is nearby. A huge rub nearby might increase your confidence, but don't think for a moment that you need this evidence to kill a big buck along a scrape line. If you know your hunting area is capable of producing a mature buck, go for it. In other words, if you can find a scrape line when the breeding is about to begin, assume that a big buck could use it just as easily as an insubordinate buck. The old-timers do not restrict themselves to certain areas once the rut arrives, and to find a doe they will want to travel the trail where the scrape line exists.

The author's scrape-line buck: a nice Indiana nine-pointer.

CHAPTER 13

Two Bucks Meet Their Destiny in the Oaks

he wind direction was favorable as I climbed into my stand, late in the archery season. Only two days of hunting remained, and although I had seen a couple of super bucks earlier in the season that didn't walk by within bow range, this morning I had new hope.

In the thick cover of a mast grove or elsewhere, a quick glance at the height of this rack might get your pulse racing, but the lack of mass, plus the buck's somewhat lean face, might suggest a younger buck best let go.

I was perched in a red oak. This tree did not produce mast, but 15 yards to the east a bigger red oak was shedding acorns consistently. I'd found the spot one day earlier, and knew from the sign around the secluded oak that it provided a good ambush opportunity. However, I had no idea that the site would produce two super whitetails in two days.

One hour after the pink sky of the morning appeared, I saw three deer coming toward the oak. They never stopped walking until they reached the acorns. They were content to dine on the bitter nuts for the next thirty minutes. The wind continued blowing from the south to the north, and I felt fortunate that none of the deer detected my presence.

Soon after the doe and fawns disappeared into a canopy of nearby honeysuckle, I saw huge white antlers bobbing up and down along a nearby valley. The buck was on a course directly to the oak. Even better, he approached from the southeast and could not scent me. He had not come to dine on the acorns, as did the doe and fawns. Instead, he concentrated on what might be there, or what had been there earlier in the morning.

My heart raced as he quartered into me less than 25 yards away. As he was about to leave the oak and continue north, he passed through an opening. I drew my bow, carefully aimed, and released. The arrow zipped through the huge buck and struck the ground. He turned and ran back from where he had come, finally disappearing over a hill.

When I recovered the buck later, I was astonished to see he carried eleven points and a double brow tine on the right antler. I later scored the buck at over 140 inches.

Although the hot oak had paid off for the archery season, I did not abandon the area. Two days later, the firearm season would begin. The acorns were still falling and I wondered if the spot could produce yet another big buck. I also thought about a certain big buck that I had spotted a week earlier, less than 300 yards from this oak. He was a super ten-pointer that had passed by at only 80 yards, and I wondered if he was still in the area.

The southerly wind direction continued for the next couple of days, and when opening morning of the gun season arrived, I headed for the same ambush site. As the hours ticked away that morning, I began to think that I had made a serious mistake in choosing this ambush site. I had seen nothing come to the acorns. I also wondered if the disturbance from getting the bow-killed buck out of the woods had played a significant role in the morning's boredom. In fact, I debated climbing down and heading for the truck, only to change my mind when I spotted a deer coming toward me.

The deer was not at all what I had hoped for. It was a lone button buck that apparently wanted to grab a few acorns before bedding down for the day. He made several loops around the oak for the next half hour. Meanwhile, I sat down and waited patiently for him to leave.

A short time later, the youngster suddenly threw up his head and stared intently to the east. I could tell that he saw something along the side of a ridge, but I saw nothing. Suddenly, the button buck turned and walked away rapidly. At first, I thought he might have spotted a hunter. I watched the hill closely, but it was not until I looked in the valley below that I saw why the young deer had left. The first thing I saw was white. Then I saw antlers, and they were wide. As I reached for my hanging gun, I tried to study the antlers to see who was about to show. Almost immediately, I knew it was the big ten-pointer that I had seen earlier during the archery season.

When the buck arrived at the oak, I nervously attempted to settle the crosshairs of the scope just behind his shoulder. But he was too close. At no more than 10 yards, I found it nearly impossible to locate an aiming point. All I could see was brown. Fortunately, before the buck got past me and angled directly away, I found the shoulder. I squeezed the trigger and the buck dropped.

The gun kill also taped out at more than 140 inches. Two super bucks in two days at one hot oak tree is uncommon, but it did happen. I won't count on a similar episode in the future, but I will continue to look for oaks that provide the best potential to intercept a big buck. (See the color insert for photos of this buck.)

The Doe Attraction

So, what made this ambush site so intriguing?

First, consider that it was late pre-rut when I killed both bucks. The peak rut was about to begin, which is why neither buck had come to feed on the acorns. Both bucks knew, however, that does were visiting the oak to feed on acorns consistently, making the spot one of the best in the area to attract a doe. Of course, it also attracted me, which led to their demise.

Secondly, consider the mast for that season. Acorns were not abundant; in fact, they were somewhat scarce. I had done plenty of scouting throughout the archery season, and while I had located a couple of other red oaks producing acorns within the same proximity, they did not provide enough mast to attract deer consistently. This red oak did. I found no white oak acorns that season. Only a few red oaks produced at all, and only one produced a good quantity of mast. Thus, it attracted several does and fawns.

There was buck sign near the oak. I could see a couple of small saplings rubbed, but they had been made at least a couple of weeks earlier. The rubs did not indicate a big buck was present, but if there's a big buck in the area, which is likely as the breeding nears, rubs mean little or nothing. It's where the does are that counts. Additionally, there were no scrapes under the oak.

A few days after I took these two bucks, my son headed for the same hot spot. The acorns were now drying up, and few does visited the site. He saw a small basket-racked ten-pointer the first morning he hunted the oak, but no other bucks in the days that followed.

The location of this oak was significant. It was located in a valley. The nearby hill was laced with deciduous trees, which included many other oaks that didn't produce mast that year. On the opposite side of the hot oak, there were small timber and thickets. This oak was isolated and quite secluded, making it an ideal location for deer to visit during daylight hours.

As for trails leading to and from the oak, there was very little evidence of any well-used routes. You could faintly see a couple

The importance of food cannot be denied, as this buck seeks a secluded patch of red oaks, just like both of the great bucks described in this chapter.

of trails, but these appeared more like seldom-traveled second-ary routes.

I hunted this same area for three more years, but never again found this particular site appealing. There was always scattered mast in the area, but the hot oak that once produced two huge bucks never again attracted deer. This is how it often works with secluded foods—they are hot one year and not the next. This is also why it's important to scout for secluded foods each season. Early in the pre-rut period, mature bucks visit them to feed during daylight hours while they roam their core areas. As the rut nears, the bucks visit the isolated foods to locate does.

CHAPTER 14

My Best Bow-Killed Buck: *A Moment of Truth*

I have always believed that you have the best chance of ambushing a super buck in an area you hunt close to home. You know this area better than others, you have more time to spend learning the habits of bucks, you have more time to hunt, and you are the one that can make things happen. Despite this theory, however, my best whitetail buck came in 1990, about 1,500 miles from my home while I was hunting the Bow Zone of Alberta, Canada. Although this book emphasizes tactical methods for taking big bucks within areas you hunt close to home, it can happen elsewhere — if it's the right area, if you use the right tactics, and if you hunt with the right individual.

It was late in the pre-rut period when I arrived to hunt a week with Jim Hole, Jr. of Classic Outfitters. The farmland regions of the archery-only area we hunted were home to several trophy whitetails. Huge rubs were common, and hunting pressure was minimal. I saw a few big bucks that week, but up until that last evening, nothing had walked within bow range.

As I walked into a tree-stand location along the fringe of an agricultural field on my final hunt, unstable winds prevailed as a front approached. Undaunted, I climbed into the stand and hoped for the best. A short time later, a few does and fawns approached en route to the field, but the wind made certain they didn't get there. It switched and the lead doe scented me. As the deer ran back in the direction from which they had come, I remembered that Jim had told me earlier that I could attempt a different tactic if the wind became unfavorable.

As soon as the antlerless deer departed, I lowered my bow and climbed down. I headed for a corner of the field that I had passed earlier. Here, the wind had seemed a bit more stable, blowing my scent into the woods behind me. Any buck that came into the field and traveled the edge would not scent me, so I settled into a natural ground blind behind three maples about 15 yards into the woods. Several scrapes and tracks bordered the edge of the field. I wasn't happy about being on the ground, but it appeared to be the only chance of bringing a wall-hanger home.

Not long before dark, and after nothing had showed, I went to work on the rattling antlers. I had carried the antlers into the stand that evening, as I had done several other times on this hunt. Jim had mentioned that rattling works quite well in this area. I did three short sequences of rattling to simulate a sparring match, each lasting about one minute, pausing for about five minutes between each sequence.

I had about given up hope as the light rapidly diminished. Then I spotted movement heading in my direction, about 60 yards down the field. Low light and the saplings around me made visibility difficult, and my first thought upon seeing gray motion was that a coyote was on its way. Coyotes were everywhere in this far north region, and it seemed likely that another encounter was about to occur. However, I had no more than relished the thought when I recognized that it was a buck. Although his antlers were dark, somehow they showed up superbly against the darkening sky. They were massive and tall, and coming directly toward me.

By the time the buck had cut our distance in half, I had already raised my bow and settled it between two of the maples. The buck walked slowly, looking into the woods for the combatants he had heard sparring. I dared not move, and I was visualizing in my mind how the buck could get past me without my being able to draw the bow. Somehow, I had to get it done before it was too late.

When the buck was directly in front of me, he stopped and gazed in my direction. He was at 20 yards, within my effective shooting range. Between us was nothing but air. There were no limbs, trees, or debris to block the shot. Unfortunately, I could not draw the bowstring. But without warning, as if it was meant to be, the buck suddenly turned his head and looked in the opposite direction across the field. Instantly, I drew, carefully took aim, and released. I heard the dull thump of the arrow striking home. The buck stumbled and then ran hard for the cover of the woods.

I stayed put until darkness arrived. Then, I cautiously left the area and headed for the road. After explaining to Jim that I was uncertain of where I had hit the buck, we decided it best to wait until morning.

At dawn the next day, we arrived and picked up an easy-to-follow blood trail leading into the woods where the buck had vanished. A short distance later, we spotted him piled up amongst the trees. The arrow had passed through his left shoulder and vital lungs. The huge-bodied buck carried twelve scorable points. Although his width was less than 16 inches, he made up for it with long brow tines and mass. He had a gross score of just under 160 inches. (See the color insert for photos of this buck.)

The Perfect Ambush Scenarios

In addition to the area itself, several factors contributed to my last-minute success. Jim knew the habits of the big bucks he pursued. He spends countless hours locating these bucks, and takes extreme precautions when setting up ambush locations (you can read about his tactics in Chapter 20).

Rattling certainly helped me to lure the buck into bow range. There was a high buck-to-doe ratio in this area, which contributed to the bucks' responsiveness to rattling. This buck had probably heard the rattling while approaching the field. It could be that he would have walked past me anyway, but that we will never know. Then there's the ground-hunting opportunity. The wind direction was wrong for the stand I'd first hunted that evening. Had I stayed there, I probably would not have left Alberta with a super buck. Up until then, I had never taken a buck on the ground with bow and arrow, and this experience provided the confidence I needed to do it again in future years.

We also know that a weather front was approaching, that evening I shot the buck. A cold front had begun moving in that afternoon, and we'd also had a little rain before I hunted. I'm sure the barometric pressure was falling, which prompted deer to move that particular evening. In fact, the following morning when we recovered the buck, the wind had stabilized out of the north as light snow fell.

Equally important was that all of Jim's ambush locations were located near the fringes of fields. Even the morning hunts had been somewhat productive near the fields, because Jim avoided disturbing big-buck hideouts. He always made certain that he didn't penetrate the area too much and interrupt the habits of super bucks. In most areas I hunt near home (and, for that matter, most areas you likely hunt), hunting along the fringes of fields will be unproductive. Hunting pressure reduces the possibility of mature bucks getting to the fields before dusk in the evenings, or walking the fringes of fields in the morning after dawn. In this area of minimal pressure, though, we could expect action some of the time in the open areas, at the same time reducing the chances of bumping a super buck into another region.

CHAPTER 15

Patterning a Pre-Rut Buck: *Second Chances with a Ten-Pointer*

T he rut was three weeks from peaking, but I felt confident that I had patterned a big buck. After locating a rub line and tying it into a bedding area and food source, I wasted no time in hanging a portable stand in a small woodlot. Although I had hunted other nearby woodlots of this farmland area during the first two weeks of the archery season, I had not seen a mature buck. Nor had I found evidence of a big buck's existence.

After setting up the promising ambush location, I headed for the truck and grabbed my bow. I would have gladly headed for the new stand, but the wind direction was totally wrong. I chose instead to hunt another stand 200 yards away. The afternoon was unproductive and I saw nothing. At dusk, I climbed down from my tree stand to head for home, still thinking about the first opportunity to hunt the new stand.

As I walked the fringe of a harvested cornfield near dark, I stayed close to cover. The last thing I wanted to do was run into the buck that had left the sign where I had placed the new stand, but my nightmare came true. After traveling only 100 yards, I spotted movement along the field's edge. Although it was twilight, I could make out heavy antlers and several points as the buck headed for the safety of the woods that I had just left.

For the rest of the evening, I silently cursed myself for what had happened. I had run right into the buck I hoped to kill. Would this one be like others, and disappear for the remainder of the hunting season?

I could only hope this mature buck did not head for parts unknown, as other home-range bucks have done in the past. On the positive side, I realized that I had not spooked the buck close to the new ambush site. Therefore, I could only wait patiently for the right day to hunt the rub line.

Though the author accidentally spooked this buck, it stuck to its home range, and a properly placed ambush site within that range later paid off.

About five days passed before the wind became favorable. My first opportunity to hunt the woodlot where the buck's sign was evident arrived on a weekend morning. I left the truck long before light and headed for the stand. It was again necessary to walk the fringe of the cornfield, and I wanted to do it during the black of night.

All went well. I arrived at the stand without incident, and the morning hunt was soon underway. About an hour after dawn, a deer—an insubordinate six-pointer—approached. He stopped only long enough to scent one of the rubs about 22 yards from the base of the tree where I was perched, then casually strolled out of sight.

The next hour passed quickly. I had nothing but squirrels to entertain me, but I still felt good about the mature buck that I had bumped into nearly a week earlier. When I spotted another deer coming, I did not realize at first that it was the big one. The deer walked very slowly with its head down, following the trail of the small buck that had passed by earlier. Several seconds passed before I spotted his dark antlers against the floor of the woods, and when I did I knew it had to be him.

I never took my eyes off the approaching buck as I reached for my hanging bow. The wind was perfect and he had been content to follow the scent of the other deer, and it seemed inevitable that he would walk past me inside bow range. I looked ahead for an opening. Then I saw the rubbed tree the small buck had scented. The buck continued approaching and when his head disappeared behind a huge oak, I drew the bow. He was in the opening near the rub in less than a heartbeat.

After releasing the arrow, one might have thought he had been shot out of a cannon, he ran that hard. He disappeared in an instant after going over a small hill, and I heard him crash to the ground.

The buck was heavy-beamed and carried ten points. He did not score as much as I had hoped, but I was nevertheless quite happy with the result. I had patterned a pre-rut buck within his home range, and it paid off. No doubt, locating the buck's area and trail contributed to the kill.

Home Range and Patterning Facts

It's worth pointing out here how dependable big bucks can be within their home range. After all, I had encountered this buck a few days earlier, yet he remained close to the area where I spooked him. This was clearly a lesson to be learned.

I've said it several times before, but it continues to bear repetition: mature bucks are seldom forgiving. After they realize your presence, most will seem to disappear. They probably don't move far, but they probably do become more cautious. Needless to say, they become far more difficult to kill than those that never know you are there. However, I don't believe that every big buck will vanish after a confrontation with a hunter. Perhaps it depends on how much the confrontation spooked them? Perhaps it depends on hunting pressure in the area, or the location? Bucks in some areas get somewhat used to human encroachment. The area where I took the ten-pointer, though, was not overrun with people. Yet, I bumped into him and sent him crashing away. He did not seem to have a curious bone in his body the evening I walked upon him. But he did remain in the area, and he did travel a trail he had traveled many times before.

The rub line in the woodlot where I shot the buck consisted of only a handful of rubs. The rubs were close together, no more than 15–20 yards apart. The secondary trail through the woodlot where I found the rubs was difficult to see. Another master trail was located in the same woodlot, no more than 100 yards from the secondary trail. The master trail was far more defined, and would probably entice many hunters to set up an ambush. The big buck, though, did not travel the master trail. He followed the secondary trail and rub line.

Consider also that this was the first time I hunted this stand. Most stand sites provide the best results the first, or perhaps the second or third, time you are there. After several hunts, you can assume the ambush site will become less productive, and this is another reason for finding several ambush locations. It's always a

This big buck senses the author's presence but can't place him. He's on high alert, yet will probably keep walking. Spook him again, and he's gone.

good idea to use different stands if you hope to keep the bucks scratching their heads.

The final aspects of analyzing this pre-rut buck relate to the bedding area and food source. The cornfield mentioned earlier, located several hundred yards from the rub line, was the food source. The nearby thicket, which I assumed was a bedding area the buck had used many times before, connected to the secondary trail.

Who knows exactly how often this buck traveled this trail? I am aware that big bucks do not walk the same route daily. I also know that I had patterned the buck within his home range, and that during the pre-rut period it's necessary to learn the whereabouts of a mature buck. Sometimes a visual sighting will lead you to a super buck before the breeding begins, and sometimes it requires extensive and cautious scouting to find a buck's core area. In my case, I did not see this buck until the evening I bumped him. The farmer had told me a couple of weeks earlier, after harvesting, that he had spotted a big buck in the cornfield. So one could say that it was a combination of a visual sighting and the scouting that led me to the buck. I knew one was in the area, and soon located the sign that allowed me to pattern him.

But even if you know a mature buck is in the area, patterning him is never easy. Learning the whereabouts of a super buck is always going to be difficult, even when you know he's there, and killing him becomes even tougher. I've patterned a number of pre-rut bucks over the years, but haven't killed many of those. Despite the obstacles, patterning a big buck is the best way to kill one before the breeding begins, and before the bucks widen their range in search of does.

CHAPTER 16

Following the Does to a Super Nine-Pointer

During the Illinois firearm season and shortly before this book headed to the editor, I selected an ambush location amongst the hardwoods and oaks. I planned my ambush in an area where acorns were abundant, and well-used trails appeared to offer the best opportunity. The rut had peaked and the bucks were on the move. The best chance of killing a mature whitetail centered on areas that does used.

Although the first morning's hunt did not go well, I returned the next morning with a favorable wind . . . or so I thought. Thirty minutes after dawn, a doe and two fawns came along a fenceline bordering the hardwoods to the west. The deer picked up my scent as it blew from the southeast to the northwest, and they vanished in less than an instant.

Nearly two hours had passed when I spotted a buck 150 yards south of me. His tall white antlers showed up clearly against the dark floor of the hardwoods. Knowing the buck would not approach closer without some prodding, I grabbed my grunt tube and went to work. However, the buck continued walking and finally disappeared over a hill.

Picking a choice spot in an area where many does traveled during the rut put the author in the path of this super buck that scored 150 inches.

I'm sure he never heard the call, but another did. Moments after the last grunt, I heard a deer approaching behind me. Slowly, I turned around and spotted the four-point buck closing ground fast. He stopped directly under me, looking intently for the buck he thought he had heard. Finally, he gave up on the idea of seeing another deer and started feeding on acorns.

After watching the buck for fifteen minutes and hoping he would move on before scenting me, I spotted movement to the south. Another deer was coming toward me, but the brush and large distance between us left me wondering. I could see antlers, but was unsure just how big the deer really was. I debated glassing him, over 100 yards away, but decided not to risk moving with the small buck under me. I also knew that the newcomer would soon be in plain view.

The young buck watched the other's every move, and I saw why. When the oncoming deer passed through a fence opening, his tall antlers became obvious. I now knew this one was a super buck, and it was headed straight for me. Slowly, I shouldered the slugster, hoping the young buck under me would not catch the movement. He didn't. Then I waited. The big buck was quartering to me sharply. When he reached the 45-yard mark, he turned broadside and began to pass by my tree stand. I picked an opening and squeezed the trigger. The buck buckled and ran hard, disappearing after a short distance.

However, before I tracked the deer—which I assumed was lethally hit—I lingered in the tree stand. During the next thirty minutes, I spotted two other bucks pass by. Neither of these were wallhangers, but they did show the effectiveness of the ambush location. By the way, the small buck that was under me had run in the same direction and directly behind the buck I had shot, before he too disappeared. However, moments later he came running back with tail flagging. I had a feeling that the huge buck had gone down.

My wife joined me some time later, and we followed the easy-to-see blood trail. We found the buck, which had run only 75 yards, within minutes. The deer carried nine points, including G-2s that taped out at 12 inches each. The G-3s were 10.5 inches each, and he carried super-long brow tines. We later scored the huge buck at 150 inches.

I saw eight deer that morning, five of which were bucks. That's often how it works when the breeding peaks. If you pattern the does effectively, you could see more bucks than antlerless deer.

Putting Together the Puzzle

The acorns factored in my success that morning, but contributed only in part to patterning the does. Almost every oak had abundant mast, and acorns were so abundant that deer could find them throughout the hardwoods. More important, the trails surrounding me became the determining factor. They were hot, and riddled with tracks and droppings. There was little in the way of buck sign, but once the rut peaks, it's the areas that does use that count the most.

The fenceline I mentioned was a natural travel corridor. Its location among the hardwoods made it hot. Early in the archery season, deer used the fenceline route only now and again. But as the acorns began falling, this route became more popular since it provided access to the abundant food source.

Another trail, which passed within 15 yards of my ambush site, meandered through the hardwoods along the side of a ridge. It, too, was riddled with sign, but its true power might have been where it led deer. Only 100 yards to the east, there was a sanctuary, grown up with brambles and honeysuckle—a preferred bedding area. Although sanctuaries are primary ambush targets both early and late in the hunting seasons, they attract deer consistently, and during the rut as well.

In the case of the big buck I shot, he was initially on the fenceline trail. He might eventually have picked up the trail that led to the sanctuary, but that we'll never know. Either way, I had both trails covered: I had the fenceline trail that bucks could travel to pick up scent of a doe that might cross the fence as it traveled to and from the hardwoods, and I also had the trail that passed through the oaks and to the sanctuary.

Before and after the breeding, I don't prefer setting up in hardwoods. In fact, I would much rather wait in ambush near the thickest cover or the secluded food sources, often along secondary travel routes. Big bucks prefer the security that only the densest cover provides. However, the bucks change their habits and take chances once the breeding begins, and that's why you must pattern the does. Hardwoods are usually somewhat open, but mature bucks fully realize that these areas provide promising opportunities for them to find does. Of course, it's the abundance of acorns that makes this possible. Normally, a limited mast allows the hunter to narrow down the areas where does and bucks will be, and in turn narrow down ambush locations. When plentiful mast exists, the hunter should locate the hottest trails passing through the acorns—those that does and fawns travel most.

During the rut, if you can find sign that does are frequenting an area or trail, then that's where you'll find the bucks that are chasing them.

CHAPTER 17

Pinpointing the Next Ambush

L ocating a huge buck and a promising ambush location several months in advance might seem impossible, but many veteran trophy hunters claim it can be done. Most rely on two tactics: post-season scouting and shed hunting. Post-season scouting allows you to find old sign that was left by previous rutting bucks. Finding sheds allows you to see "who" survived the rut. Both methods are enjoyable and provide an opportunity to be in the woods at a time of the year when you don't risk spooking a buck into an area you don't hunt.

During late winter and early spring, the bucks are back in their home range. This is the primary reason that post-season scouting and shed hunting can be beneficial, and you can combine both tactics in one outing on a favorable winter day. Alternatively, if you are a spring turkey hunter, you can spend a few of the day's off-hours gaining ground for next autumn's trophy deer hunt.

Those Amazing Sheds

Hunting sheds is nothing new. Native Americans as well as pioneers often searched for deer antlers for a variety of purposes. Although sheds are sought by collectors and used by many folks today for making decorative items, many hunters seek them just to know who survived the previous hunting season. Here's how it works: find an antler that came from a two-and-a-half-year-old buck, and you know that a three-and-a-half-year-old will be there next year. Find a three-and-a-half-year-old's antler, and—well, you get the picture. The buck that sheds the antler will probably sport larger antlers the following season. You also know that the area where you found the antler is located within the buck's home range and that he will likely be near during the next hunting season.

Scanning the ground and treelines for shed antlers takes time but can be very informative. And if they indicate trophy status, that is proof positive that there's a super buck in the area that survived yet another hunting season.

The time of year you pursue antlers is vital to your success. Looking too soon, before most bucks have shed, could dampen your spirits before making another attempt. Looking too late could mean finding distorted antlers. For instance, looking in areas with a large number of smaller animals that love to gnaw on bone could mean finding an antler with points shorter than original. Terrain and weather can also affect your chances of locating a shed. In bottomlands, water and debris might take their toll on antlers before you get to them. It's therefore important to know when bucks shed in your area, and to time your hunts accordingly.

Throughout most of North America, many bucks shed in February. Some drop antlers in January, and quite a few still carry antlers in March. Rarely do I spot bucks in late December that have already shed one antler, or see bucks in April with both antlers. On balance, I prefer to do most of my shed hunting in late March or early April when I can count on most antlers to have hit the ground.

I would not suggest you head for the woods with a bushel basket. Sheds are not necessarily easy to see, and you should never count on an abundance of antlers in any given area. Antler hunting requires time, dedication, and some knowledge of the best areas to search.

Consider a buck I observed from my vehicle for about fifteen minutes. The one-antlered buck fed on honeysuckle about 80 yards from the road. Eventually, he walked into a denser thicket and disappeared, only to reappear along the edge of the road a few minutes later. The one antler he carried was gone. With binoculars, I could plainly see a bloody spot on the pedicle and realized he had just shed the antler during the short period he had vanished. As soon as the buck crossed the road, I wasted no time heading for the thicket to search for the antler. Because I could see the thicket where the buck had shed, I assumed I would be back to the vehicle with the antler very quickly, but it took nearly an hour of painstaking searching before I spotted the antler lying on the ground below a tangle of briars.

Although random searching is most effective, it still requires considerable time. Random searching means walking an area back and forth. By being systematic, you can be more certain of not missing an antler, and know you covered the area completely.

Last year, I saw a huge buck on two occasions in late winter. The hunting seasons had ended and I was thrilled to know this buck had survived. The first time I saw him, he carried both antlers. When I saw him three weeks later, he had only one. Two weeks after that, I headed for the woods with hopes of finding his

Because bucks are in their home range when they shed their antlers, a shed lets you know exactly who will be around during the next season before the breeding begins.

beautiful sheds. I spent three days searching his home range, but never found one of the antlers.

Seldom do you spot antlers from great distances. Even the largest and whitest sheds can be difficult to see. Binoculars will help, since you can view white objects without walking out of your way. However, I locate most antlers within a few yards of where I walk. For this reason, I stay focused on the ground within 20 yards of my location. On one occasion, I spotted an antler from about 30 yards, but it was a huge antler hooked over a branch about three feet above the ground.

Most hunters walk trails, or search food sources and bedding areas. It would be difficult for me to say which offers the best opportunity. If one field is attracting deer, you can assume that deer are spending time there. The longer they dwell there, the better the chance they will drop an antler. Nevertheless, searching a large field can be very time-consuming. On one occasion, I located a shed antler nearly 100 yards away while glassing a field. However, this was a green field and the stubbles were only a few inches above the ground.

My best results have come from searching bedding areas and along trails. The key is to make certain you search active areas. It is common sense not to shed hunt when snow is on the ground, although snow does show you the areas deer use most. Natural travel routes and funnels that connect with bedding areas and food sources are ideal locations. This could be a narrow woods, thicket, ditch, or fenceline.

Finding a matched set of sheds is seldom easy. I've done it a few times, but only because the buck dropped both antlers at or near the same location. Although I have tried, I have never found matching sheds a long distance apart. A couple of years ago, a friend of mine did so. The buck was a ten-pointer, and three weeks elapsed after the hunter found one before he located the other, about a quarter mile away.

I'm unsure why some bucks will shed both antlers at the same time while others will shed one antler and not the other until days or weeks later. There's no reason to believe that it's genetically related, either. I know of a pen-reared buck that shed both antlers at the same moment when he was six-and-a-half years old. I found his antlers while photographing the deer in the four-acre enclosure, but that was the only time the buck ever shed his antlers together. During other years, he typically shed one antler and did not drop the other until several days later.

Although some bucks shed their antlers at the same moment, many drop only one and carry the other for several days or weeks before it, too, falls off.

Although I've heard some folks claim that big bucks shed earlier than little bucks, I'm not so sure. Researchers have claimed that bucks in good physical shape might shed later than those in poor condition. But I do believe that the same buck will shed his antlers close to the same time each year. The pen-reared buck mentioned previously always shed his antlers in mid-February. He was the breeding buck and probably not in as good condition as others in the enclosure. He usually shed between the eighth and twentieth day of the month. I've also heard from others who have raised deer that certain bucks seem to shed about the same time each year. Thus, we might postulate that there's no given time when all bucks will shed, but there is a period when one certain buck might shed.

Post-Season Scouting

In one way, shed hunting is a lot like tracking a wounded deer—you often cover lots of ground, and you observe many things you might not have otherwise. I can't tell you how many times I have found great areas to ambush a buck while following a blood trail. You are far more observant when you focus on what's right in front of your nose. The same principle applies when I hunt for sheds, thereby making it a beneficial post-season scouting adventure which helps me to find old rubs and scrapes, and super travel routes.

There's an important difference between locating sheds and locating buck sign, however. As mentioned earlier, sheds provide proof of a big buck's existence, whereas locating old buck sign does not. In fact, the buck that left the sign might no longer be in this world. Nevertheless, there is a positive side of locating old buck sign. Both rubs and scrapes tell you where bucks have been, and where a buck could be next season.

We saw in Chapter 11 that rub lines provide ambushing opportunities, particularly before the breeding begins when many bucks are in their home range. It's important to keep in mind that rub lines seldom appear randomly. Most seem to appear in the same general vicinities year after year, and there is a simple reason for this: some areas are attractive to bucks each season. These areas will continue to attract bucks as long as it retains its attractive characteristics. Even if the buck or bucks that once walked the rub line are now in the freezer, you can bet that more bucks and another rub line will show up nearby.

Old rubs are not as easy to locate as fresh rubs, and you can expect the older rubs to appear much darker than they once did. The benefit of locating an old rub line is that you can do so at a time of the year when you can cover it vigilantly. If you cover an area thoroughly and locate rub lines during the hunting season, you risk spooking a big buck out of the area.

Old scrapes can remain visible months after the breeding ends. Usually it's best to search for them before the green-up begins in spring. You can search for either sporadic scrapes, or scrape lines that could provide potential the following season. The benefit of finding an individual scrape is that you can check it as the season progresses during the upcoming hunting season. Some scrapes will appear season after season in the same location under the same trees, and you can mark off those scrapes that are not renewed the following year.

Scrapes that offer the most opportunity are those with sign above the ground. The largest scrapes might appear the most promising, but those most likely to reoccur during the next rut are the ones that show evidence of broken limbs above the scrape. I have found, however, that some reoccurring scrapes will die once too much damage occurs to the limbs above the scrape.

The post-season provides the best time to select ambush locations and clear shooting lanes. Every deer in the area has plenty of time to get used to changes. You might have to make a few adjustments after the foliage appears, but you can complete most of the work and disturbance long before it would have a detrimental effect.

Keep in mind that post-season scouting and shed hunting is part of the ambush. It might not appear as such, since the hunting is months away, but I suggest you take it seriously. Some may find it more difficult to grasp than other methods discussed in this book, simply because you can't apply the results immediately. But make no mistake, the more you learn about a buck, the better the chance you will meet him up close and personal.

CHAPTER 18

Ambush Errors:
The Biggest Mistakes and What They Taught Me

We've all heard the old saying, "Fool me once, shame on you. Fool me twice, shame on me." And we all understand the gist of this phrase and how it applies to everyday life. It can also apply to ambushing trophy whitetails. You might get by with fooling a big buck once, but you're unlikely to fool him twice.

In case we haven't hammered it enough yet: big bucks are seldom forgiving. They learn from their mistakes. Moreover, they learn from your mistakes. Your errors will make certain you don't have a close encounter with a mature whitetail, despite all you know about a buck and the tactics that can fool him. No hunter can possibly avoid making errors, but we can limit those that will cost us shooting opportunities. Here's a look at the biggest mistakes we make, and an analysis of those from which I have learned.

Hunting a "Dead" Food Source

I can still remember a tremendous ambush location that was situated 75 yards from a harvested cornfield. The first time I hunted the stand, I saw five bucks. One qualified as a trophy, but passed me 50 yards beyond my effective shooting range.

The landowner had harvested the field about three days before I set up a portable stand. It was the early archery season and the deer had hammered the field each evening. Along the fringe of the field's north side was a long, dense section of honeysuckle and blackberry briars. At least one rub line was noticeable close to the field within the thicket, which was where I set up the blind.

I tried again a few days later, and saw a two-year-old that I had also spotted during my first hunt there. Then I saw a small buck several days later. I stuck with the blind for the next couple of weeks whenever the wind remained favorable, but the buck sightings stopped. Meanwhile, I wasted valuable hunting time that might have paid off elsewhere.

It's no big news that many hunters kill trophy whitetails near food sources each season. But it's also no big news that food sources die quickly. Unfortunately, for the brief period when they are hot, they keep us tied down and unwilling to leave. It could be an agricultural field that dies shortly after it's hot, or it could be a secluded food source, such as persimmons or acorns.

For nearly two weeks I hunted a dead cornfield. True, deer occasionally visited the field, but my chances of killing a mature whitetail near this food source dwindled rapidly. I was there when it was hot, but remained there after it died. No food source lasts throughout the hunting season, although some foods last longer than others do. The time you waste near a food source that no longer produces action will cost you. Some foods stop attracting big bucks when the food is no longer available, but many fail to attract big bucks after they have been hunted a few times. (The latter also relates to the multi-stand approach discussed previously.) Mature bucks will not consistently go to the same food source. After showing up a time or two, they are far more reluctant about coming than does and insubordinate bucks are. It's almost as though they want to keep you guessing.

We know that ambushing a trophy whitetail requires us to hunt the most promising locations, but the time involved is limited. The moment a food source dies, it's time to move on. Perhaps

Knowledge of secondary trails can be important, as oftentimes big bucks will leave the primary trails to the does and young bucks.

you will need to hunt a secondary trail. Perhaps you will need to scout for a promising rub line. Alternatively, you might have to seek out another food source. Always remember that when you locate a promising food source, it is promising for only a short time.

Knowing when to move on is seldom difficult—if all deer stop coming to the food source, you can bet it's over. I look at it another way: once I've hunted the location a few times, the chance that a big buck will show becomes very unlikely.

Hunting Only Big-Buck Sign

Some hunters claim that some writers attempt to make a science out of buck sign. These hunters suggest that it's best to leave the research factors out when it comes to ambushing a super whitetail. I agree that science can sometimes be misleading, and that veteran whitetail hunters learn far more from hunting big bucks than they do from reading scientific treatises on them. I won't deny that research tells us plenty about why bucks make rubs and scrapes, and how to determine a big buck was responsible, but I've concluded that too many hunters worry about setting up ambush locations only near sign where a big buck has been. Bucks are bucks. Any way you look at it, age doesn't really matter when it comes to bucks rubbing and scraping. Rub lines and scrapes that attract little bucks also attract big bucks.

Many years ago when I first began pursuing trophy whitetails, I often limited ambush locations to areas where I found big-buck sign. I believed it was necessary to find the biggest rubs, the biggest tracks, and scrapes that showed some indication that a super whitetail had been there. I soon learned that this was a grave error. Granted, I still love finding huge trees shredded to pieces, and big tracks, but I don't rely on setting up ambush locations only where a big buck has been. Any area that attracts little bucks could also attract big bucks.

I've often heard hunters discuss finding big buck tracks. I agree that some big bucks leave big tracks. However, big-bodied bucks with smaller racks also leave big tracks. Tracks have nothing to do with antlers. Thus, I suggest you never determine an ambush location's potential based on nearby track size. During the rut, when you must pattern does to find big bucks, numerous tracks mean far more than big tracks. Early in the season, when you must pattern big bucks, a rub line of small rubbed trees could mean more than big tracks do.

Although timing of rubs and scrapes is vital to your ambush-site-producing action, the area where they are located will have far more to do with success than do rub and track size. If you set up in the right area when rubs are active, you have a chance of a big buck showing, even if you found only small rubs. If you set up in the right area near scrapes late in the pre-rut when they are active, a mature buck could appear, despite the apparent absence of large tracks. The right areas are those that provide big bucks with security. Early in the hunting season before pressure accelerates, the right areas could be a short distance from an agricultural field. Late in the season, the right areas are often along the fringes of the thickest cover we often refer to as whitetail sanctuaries.

In summary, I suggest you never focus your ambush locations on only big-buck sign. Little bucks often lead you to big bucks.

Sure, it's wonderful if you do find big-buck sign, and it provides confidence, but that's not the bottom line. Deer are creatures of habit. Areas that appeal to little bucks will also appeal to them as they mature. Big bucks might not take as many chances as little bucks—they are more cautious and they possess stronger survival instincts—but the big boys tread over the same ground as do the smaller guys.

Scouting Errors

Many ambush sites are spoiled before the hunt begins. In fact, some hunters ruin ambush locations before they even select them. Consider one of my scouting endeavors that occurred several years ago in southern Indiana. Two weeks before the hunting season, I noisily walked through a 40-acre tract of timber and thickets, searching for sign. I found plenty, and even made a positive ID on a huge buck that headed for the next county. I felt very discouraged and knew I had made a serious error, but I hoped the tall-antlered buck would return. He did. When I returned three days later to set up a portable stand, I jumped the same buck again, 150 yards from where he flushed the first time. I set up the stand anyway. I even hunted the ambush site a few more times before I got the message that this buck had vanished.

I have talked previously about bumping into a couple of bucks and how they returned to the same area, but that's a rarity. Also, consider that scouting for a big buck is extremely sensitive business. Regardless of whether you know he exists before you scout, you can be certain there is no chance of intercepting him when you want to, if you apply the wrong methods while you're scouting.

Many farmland hunters absolutely refuse to penetrate far on foot. They do most of their scouting by way of vehicle. They drive roads at opportune times and glass agricultural fields. Some learn the whereabouts of mature bucks. Although a few hunters might think this is a lethargic method, it can actually be quite effective if opportunity allows. Vehicles sometimes spook big bucks, but not the same way that hunters on foot do. But it won't always work well, and this method of scouting is primarily limited to the early archery season before hunting begins.

As the hunting season progresses, it isn't always possible to scout by way of vehicle. I do a portion of my scouting using this method, but much is done the old-fashioned way. Scouting from vehicles doesn't show you rub lines, hot scrapes, secluded foods, or the best trails. After having been through the scouting school of hard knocks, I have learned valuable lessons for scouting on foot, which has helped me to find and kill big bucks.

Scouting is necessary to find big-buck ambush sites, but I suggest you do it only on the right days. Windy days are ideal since you can move about with the least amount of disturbance. I prefer walking just before rain arrives. Providing the weatherman's prediction is on target, I can count on my scent to be eliminated.

It's also advisable to scout during midday hours when big bucks are least likely to be up and moving. Cooler temperatures early in the morning might be more attractive, but it's better to sweat a little, and swat mosquitoes and gnats, than to confront a super buck that's out and about.

Avoid the densest cover whenever you penetrate the area. It's okay to get near, but remain a safe distance away, and never be tempted to go inside a dense area and have a look around. I never made the mistake again of walking into the 40-acre thicket where I flushed the big buck twice. I walked the fringes of this dense area, but I always avoided going in and looking around.

I am convinced that many big-buck ambush locations don't pay off only because the hunter spoiled them in advance of the hunt. Many sites have great potential, but not if you overdo your efforts to find the site. When scouting for the right ambush location, I suggest you don't always make it a point to set up along the hottest-looking trail between the bedding area and food source. That's not to say that such a location might not help you to ambush a mature whitetail, but this old traditional strategy has long been mentioned for killing deer in general, not just big bucks. Finally, simplify your scouting periods by keeping them brief. Locate secondary trails, the densest cover, buck sign, and food sources that are active, but always avoid walking into possible bedding areas.

The Big One: Your Scent

I consider the dispersal of human scent the number-one error committed by hunters. I'm very paranoid when it comes to scent and precautions, probably because it has cost me several big bucks over the years. I believe that every serious trophy whitetail hunter will agree that you can't be too cautious.

I won't get into the basics of hunting only where the wind is favorable. You already know the importance of selecting the ambush location that won't get you into odor trouble. But hunting where the wind is always favorable does not make certain you remain in the clear. More big bucks are saved because of their nose than for any other reason. Not a season goes by that I am not scented by deer, and many big bucks have escaped a deadly encounter because they smelled me before the ambush occurred. The good news is that I have learned a few ways to get past a big buck's nose. I also have learned how to correct things once a big buck detects my presence. These methods have helped me to kill more big bucks in recent years.

Variable winds are common, and we often experience these when fronts approach. You already know the importance of hunting when the barometer crashes as a front approaches, but the variable winds that accompany a front can promptly get you into trouble. You know how it works. First, there is a southerly wind. Without warning it switches to the west, or turns totally around and comes from the north. Meanwhile, if a huge buck walks slowly as he approaches, you can bet the inconsistent wind will be your demise.

Some ambush locations offer the best opportunity when a variable wind exists. For example, an inconsistent wind is the least troublesome in open areas, such as a fenceline, funnel, or bottleneck that has openings on both sides. Such an area might not necessarily be the most attractive to a big buck, but it is where you will have the best chance of beating a variable wind. When

Dealing with wind direction is absolutely critical. Blow this one and there's a good chance you've blown your hunt.

setting up ambush locations with a nose for consistent wind direction, be aware that hills and hollows can make the blows inconsistent. Air currents often bounce off a hill and change direction. Many years ago when I used to hunt old strip-mined areas where 30–40-foot hills were everywhere, I often found it nearly impossible to beat the wind if I didn't hunt on top. A breeze from the south could hit a hill to the north and end up bouncing to the east or west. That area cost me a big buck late one evening as it approached my stand. I learned quickly, though, and made it a point to set up along the highest ground where the winds were more dependable.

I believe some trophy hunters rely too much on scent-eliminating clothing and cover scents to fool a big buck's nose. I sometimes wear scent-eliminating clothing but have never come to believe it will always save me. Such apparel helps if a big buck passes through a crosswind, but if the same buck approaches with the wind in his face, you are probably in trouble. I seldom use cover scents, except in areas where I have attempted to smell like the surroundings. Covering up human scent is a difficult, and sometimes impossible, task.

I believe you should put more emphasis on prevention of scent around your ambush site. This is far more important than attempting to mask human scent, which when left on debris close to a tree stand or ground blind will stick around for a while. It's there after you leave, and will let a big buck know where you've been . . . and where you'll be. In some areas, I have noticed that some does and fawns become accustomed to my scent, becoming less fearful as the season progresses. However, I don't see this happening with mature bucks.

One last factor should be considered. If a big buck detects your scent, I suggest you don't stick with the ambush site and wait on the same buck to return. He could, but it's unlikely. Moving your ambush site only 100 yards could make a big difference. I still remember a huge early-season buck that scented me when he approached from the direction opposite from the one I'd anticipated. He didn't stick around and ask questions. One whiff, and he vanished. I moved my portable tree stand the following day only 75 yards. A few days later, I spotted the same buck come out of the same thicket. He stopped and glared toward the area where he had scented me the first time. After a minute, he walked away and totally avoided my previous ambush site. He did not come within bow range of my new stand, but I learned first-hand that big bucks don't forget. For this reason, if you are scented by a big buck, don't put off the task of moving your ambush site. Do it immediately. Why sit in a dead zone when the action might be a mere stone's throw away?

Human scent is most costly in a big buck's home range, during early and late seasons when they know every bush and sapling of the area, and when they travel within their core area daily.

CHAPTER 19

Big Bucks Make Mistakes, Too: *How to Tip the Hunt in Your Favor*

T hroughout this book, you have read about numerous advanced, tactical solutions for tagging huge bucks—perhaps so many that it seems overwhelming, and impracticable to accomplish. Relax, and don't think for a moment that you must employ each and every strategy to kill a wall-hanger.

I won't go as far as saying that this book has made a mountain out of a molehill. On the contrary, it does require some effort and expertise to consistently kill big bucks. The more you know about big bucks, the better. Nevertheless, each hunting season many monster bucks fall to hunters who didn't apply highly evolved techniques. Many of these folks were not die-hard hunters who spent every waking moment in the woods. Many are not individuals who understand the habits of big bucks. Many are not hunters who hunt only the best places where most mature bucks congregate. Each year, you hear stories of guys who headed for the deer woods ready to shoot any deer to fill the freezer, but came home with an unbelievable buck. Some of these are tales of luck. You know how it works: a hunter walks into the woods, sits on a stump, and the first deer to walk by is a ten-point buck with a 20-inch spread.

Consider this: I have taken numerous big bucks with bow and gun, yet I have never taken a Boone-and-Crockett buck. I have killed several that surpassed the Pope-and-Young minimum score, and a couple that came close with gross scores of near 160, but not once have I came out of the woods with a buck that surpassed the Boone and Crockett 170-inch minimum score. On the other hand, there are folks out there whose first buck easily topped 170 inches. Yes, it can happen without knowing anything at all about big bucks.

Yes, large bucks can do foolhardy things during breeding season, like making a break for it across an open field just at dusk. Does he know you're hesitating because you're not sure legal shooting hours are over?

The Quick Turnaround

Tim Hilsmeyer once told me that it only takes one minute to turn around. You can hunt hard all season, or you can hunt only one day, but no matter how discouraged you are, and no matter how late in the season it becomes, the right buck could suddenly appear. This conversation occurred one day over the telephone as I complained about not seeing any mature bucks, and it helped to keep me going. In fact, it was only a few days later that I took a huge ten-pointer. This late-season buck (previously mentioned in Chapter 2) was killed a few weeks after the peak rut when it seemed time had run out. I had hunted hard throughout the early archery and firearm season, but to no avail. When I sat in my portable stand that morning, I had little faith that I would come home with a big buck, but nevertheless it happened. One minute earlier, I had not seen a deer. One minute later, the buck was coming and on a direct course with destiny.

The best time period in which you may hope to catch a super buck in a mistake is the peak rut. I know of one individual who set up a tree stand in the middle of a two-acre thicket of multiflora roses and sumacs. It's a primary bedding area, which I discovered while shed hunting in late winter. Woods surround this ideal sanctuary on three sides. There are fabulous trails coming in and out, and the guy could have easily set up along the fringe of the bedding area without penetrating it and risking running deer out. Nevertheless, for whatever reason he planned his ambush in the middle of the thicket.

Although the ambush site would probably not pay off during the pre-rut period or late season when bucks are within their home range, it could happen during the rut. Who's to say that a mature buck might not come trooping through the sanctuary at any time of day to search for a doe?

When breeding begins, bucks do crazy things. Hunters don't have to know everything there is about hunting them to be successful. I've always said that more bucks are killed because they did something wrong, and not because the hunter did something right. That's not to say that you might not deserve a big one, or

The breeding imperative occupies most of a
buck's consciousness during the rut, making him
more oblivious to other factors – like hunter error.

that you didn't do a little something right to make it happen. I'm just saying that during the rut, you don't have to be that knowledgeable a big-buck hunter for it to happen. A mature buck is often responsible for his own demise. He makes a mistake, and you take advantage of it when it happens.

Every Minute Counts

I also believe that the harder you hunt, the luckier you get. If you are out there, something good could happen. You can't kill one while you sit in front of the television with a bowl of popcorn in your lap, but you could kill one if you are waiting in ambush, even if it's not an ideal location. It's called staying power. The longer you are on stand when the breeding occurs, the better your chance of seeing a whopper buck.

Some folks hunt all their life and never kill a buck that scores better than 125 inches. Let's assume that this measurement qualifies a buck as a mature deer, and one that is three-and-a-half years old or more. Some hunters are fortunate enough to reside close to big-buck areas, but we can't deny that those who consistently kill big bucks usually have a sound knowledge of a big buck's habits, and they hunt hard. The latter is probably just as important as understanding mature bucks. Again, the more you are out there, the better the chance it can happen.

That brings up another point. Even those who can hunt only on weekends could be considered hard hunters. For this reason, you should give any ambush location a fair chance to produce.

I've discussed multi-stand tactics to keep bucks guessing, but that doesn't mean that you should give up on a certain ambush site too quickly. Many hunters, upon not seeing deer, or the right buck, will forfeit a specific location and move on to what they believe is greener grass. They assume it is the wrong spot, when in fact it might be the best location if it's given a fair shake. This must be balanced, of course, against the timeliness factor that we discussed in the previous chapter.

Surprises and Luck

It's also best if you don't believe that you must hunt a particular big buck in order to kill one. Most big bucks that are killed were not viewed on numerous occasions and studied by the individuals who shot them. More often than not, when a hunter does kill a big buck, he or she had never seen him previously, nor did they know he existed. Hunters who take big bucks consistently seldom hunt for and rely on shooting one certain buck. It does happen, but most dedicated trophy hunters count on finding sign and areas attractive to big bucks, and patterning the does during the rut. When and if they kill a super buck, odds are they had never seen him before.

Lastly, many trophy hunters also rely on luck. I've never felt very lucky, and I've always felt like I have to work hard for success. Perhaps that's human nature and we all feel that way. Nevertheless, as rare as it may be, I enjoy getting lucky when it happens. I believe that most of the time I have to do something right to take advantage of luck, but luck has contributed more than once. The eight-pointer mentioned in Chapter 3 was about to pass by me. It was late in the morning and I was close to giving it up. Fortunately, I remained on stand for an additional few minutes. It took a grunt tube to place the big buck in bow range, but luck certainly played a role.

I suggest that you always head for the woods thinking that luck could contribute to you killing a monster buck. You and I both know that Lady Luck might not assist, but we also know that the possibility exists. There are no statistics we can refer to for how often luck applies to killing a super whitetail, but you can assume that luck kills far more big bucks each season than do educated hunters.

CHAPTER 20

Secrets of the Pros

Throughout this book you've read about a variety of strategies to ambush trophy whitetails. Some probably interested you more, and some probably made more sense than others. I attempted to cover those that are most important, and those that have helped me to enjoy success. The one thing we know for sure is that it usually takes a number of tactics to be successful. I believe every veteran whitetail hunter will attest to that fact, and that each geographical region requires different strategies. Here's what some of the pros of North America have to say:

Gabe Shaffner *(an avid Midwestern bowhunter since the 1960s, pro-staffer for PSE Archery since 1995, with several huge bucks to his credit)*

Shaffner suggests every serious hunter learn their area and first make sure a big buck exists. Then it's time to decipher how and where it moves. He recommends spending as much time as possible in the field, since it can sometimes take years of hunting one area to learn the habits of big bucks.

"Shed hunting has been a tremendous asset for me," said Shaffner. "You can learn more about your area, and find a big buck's core area. And if you find sheds, you know the same big buck will be there during the next hunting season."

Consider a huge 167-inch buck taken by Shaffner in 2004. He had located the deer's shed antlers months earlier, less than a quarter mile from where he killed the deer. In the early 1990s, Shaffner located sheds of another huge buck for three straight years. This required considerable effort, but soon led to him harvesting the buck, whose antlers surpassed 180 inches.

Finally, Shaffner noted that big whitetail bucks are very different from any other animal, and that they will not take excessive pressure. For this reason, he makes it a point to set up numerous tree stands. This allows him to always hunt where the wind is favorable, and to avoid overhunting any given area. He claims that the hunter should never stick to the same location and hunt it repeatedly—his belief is that big bucks will discover quickly that they are the hunted. Shaffner will hunt a location once or twice and then allow a cooling period before returning.

Jay Cassell (*Deputy Editor of* Field & Stream *magazine, avid hunter in the northeastern and southern U.S. and Québec, Canada*)

Cassell notes that weather and time of year influence his primary hunting tactics for big bucks. During the pre-rut and peak rut, he relies on tried-and-true stand sites that he has identified season-after-season, always making certain wind direction is suitable. He avoids taking chances when the wind is wrong, and for this reason relies on several proven stand sites that he has established over the years. Additionally, if the right opportunity exists, he often resorts to another form of ambush: still-hunting.

"Not only does still-hunting require the hunter to have his senses on full alert 100 percent of the time, but it tests your knowledge, forcing you to rely on all of your senses as well as on your experience," explained Cassell.

Cassell particularly enjoys still-hunting throughout the peak rut, when big bucks know that the hunting is on. He claims this is when they head for cover and lay up until dark, moving only to feed briefly or follow an estrous doe. He also said that he prefers to still-hunt when the ground is moist, and usually follows terrain that dampens his footfalls and along waterways that drown his approach. However, Cassell said that surprising a big buck when still-hunting requires essential pre-season scouting to know where they bed and eat, and this is easier when the hunter sticks to areas he knows best. Cassell's final recommendation is to move slowly; if you think you're moving too slowly, you probably aren't moving slowly enough.

Tim Hilsmeyer (*an avid Midwestern hunter with bow and gun for more than forty years, credited with several Pope-and-Young-caliber bucks*)

"Learning the terrain and knowing a buck's habits has to be stored in your memory bank," explained Hilsmeyer. "You have to know where he goes, where he feeds, and where he beds."

He also said that many hunters do effectively learn their hunting area and pattern big bucks, but soon discover how easily they can blow a shooting opportunity the moment they could have

Southern Indiana hunter Tim Hilsmeyer got his trophy whitetail by knowing every inch of the portion of the buck's home range that he hunted, leaving no hiding place to guesswork.

successfully ambushed the deer. "Lots of hunters do everything right, like hunting where the wind is favorable and setting up a stand in the right location. But you have to be able to close the deal. As soon as you spot a buck you know you want to shoot—this is the time when you have to do everything right."

He said there are several important factors, such as controlling your emotions when a big buck appears, and knowing when to shoot. For instance, you should forget about scoring a buck when he's on the hoof. If instinct tells you it is a buck to shoot, take your eyes off the antlers and concentrate on the first opportunity to make a killing shot. He claims that experience is most helpful, and that it's absolutely normal for your heart rate to accelerate. However, to get the job done one must apply the necessary concentration, and do what's necessary to make certain to get the killing shot. This could mean luring a buck closer with a call, or making a sound at the right moment to get a moving buck to stop.

Peter Fiduccia *(an avid hunter of the Northeast and New England states, host of "Woods N' Water" TV series, book author, known as the "Deer Doctor")*

Fiduccia claims that using "unorthodox" strategies has contributed to his successes. He enjoys using odd decoys, doing as little walking as possible to scout in the area he hunts, and hunting the off-hours.

"To score on big bucks year after year, hunters have to learn to use the element of surprise," noted Fiduccia. "Once a buck reaches three-and-a-half years of age, he becomes extremely sensitive to unusual movement in his favorite haunts—so much so, that he will become even more secretive than normal. Once I am familiar with a spot I want to hunt, I refrain from going into the woods to look for sign. Instead, I scout from my vehicle with binoculars or by using game cameras that I set up when I do my first inspection of the land I intend to hunt."

Fiduccia points out that making visible sightings of bucks is often better than finding sign, providing it can be done by glassing fields. He drives the back roads and watches fields until he is able to see a big buck. This alleviates the possibility of the buck detecting the hunter, while the hunter discovers precisely the area the big buck utilizes.

As for setting up game cameras, Fiduccia penetrates the area cautiously, placing the cameras along two different types of trails.

He sets one up along a major runway to see antlerless deer and determine the buck-to-doe ratio of the area. However, he prefers the less noticeable and more concealed trails to find mature bucks. "This tactic helps me to quickly learn what size resident bucks I have on the farm," explained Fiduccia.

When decoying, Fiduccia prefers offbeat items to stop or lure bucks into range. For instance, he uses a natural doe tail hung over a limb, 26–28 inches high, to give the illusion of a deer's tail. He then attaches a 30-yard piece of green cord so that he can make it move, and he reports phenomenal results. He also places plastic apples soaked in apple scent, or plastic corn soaked in corn scent, on the ground.

Peter claims his most successful tactic is to hunt big bucks from 9:30 A.M. to 2:00 P.M., and then move to another location for the evening hunt. He claims this method is far more effective than spending the day at a single stand. "Big bucks feel most comfortable moving about during the off-hours when the hunting pressure decreases, and particularly late in the season," said Fiduccia.

Jeff Hintz *(an avid deer hunter for more than thirty years, credited with several huge whitetails taken in Montana)*

Ambushing a super buck by way of a tree stand can be tough business in the West. Hintz claims that because of vast, dense vegetation and winds that are consistently variable, he has enjoyed positive results still-hunting.

"It's easy in this country [the West] to sit in a tree stand and miss out on the action," said Hintz. "You could have several bucks after a doe just a short distance away and miss it all. Still-hunting gives you the opportunity to find the action and the big bucks. And when the wind changes directions, you can also change directions to compensate."

To still-hunt successfully, Hintz said you can't move too slowly. For instance, he might spend an hour moving only 100 yards. Nevertheless, he often relies on calls and rattling to bring bucks to him. When rattling, he looks for natural travel corridors where bucks can approach downwind; he claims that most prefer to circle and come in with the wind in their nose. For this reason, he sets up where visibility is favorable to him.

Although Hintz enjoys the best results rattling during the pre-rut period (usually within one week of the peak rut), he suggests you don't limit your rattling to this time. He has also enjoyed success when the breeding peaks and during the post-rut period.

Jim Hole, Jr. (operator of Classic Outfitters (www.classic-outfitters.com) since 1984, specializing in archery-only, trophy whitetail hunting)

"I believe a hunter should first look for areas with the least amount of pressure," said Hole. "The lower the harvest, the more big bucks available. The harder the area is hunted, the more difficult it becomes to get close to these animals."

As for hunting methods, Hole says it's vital to use conservative tactics to find out what the bucks are doing—without getting in the middle of them. "One of the biggest mistakes hunters make is getting into areas where big bucks are already moving freely. Bucks that are not aware of pressure already have moving patterns that are loose, making them vulnerable. Once they [bucks] become aware they are being hunted, it is a whole new world, and the hunting becomes so much more difficult."

Hole said the key to beating a big buck in his area is to find quality areas. He suggests that hunters remain extremely cautious when scouting a buck's range and learning his habits, remaining clear of the animal as much as you can. Once the hunter does seem to get a handle on a buck's movements, he claims you should hunt the deer only when steady winds occur.

Lastly, Hole suggested that each hunter should differentiate between deer hunting and trophy hunting. "You must remember that trophy animals are mature animals; mature means experience; experience means low tolerance; low tolerance means you must be organized and really on top of things in order to penetrate the fine-tuned defenses of a big buck."

Eddie Salter *(Public relations manager of Hunter's Specialties, avid bowhunter of the South for many years, credited with several mature bucks)*

"I started hunting with dogs and eventually participated in drives," explained Salter. "But once it seemed like it wasn't a challenge, I started bowhunting for big bucks from a tree stand. Then I found out it was an entire different element, and I began to rely on calls and different tactics to bring big bucks in close."

Nevertheless, Salter believes that scouting is most important for locating trophy whitetails. In fact, he discovered that his spring turkey-hunting experiences have contributed most to locating big bucks. Although he has relied on post-season scouting during turkey season in the South, he recalls a recent turkey hunt

Long days of spring scouting led Eddie Salter to this huge Iowa buck, taping at more than 180 inches.

to Iowa that allowed him to take his best deer ever when he returned to the area during the fall—a huge buck that taped out at over 180 inches. Salter said that while scouting in spring, he found the necessary sign that led him to return months later.

During spring, Salter looks for food sources and trails that might have potential in the fall. He seriously looks at old buck sign, and pays particular attention to scrapes. However, because he also believes that you can severely spook mature bucks, he selects tree-stand sites at that time as well, so that when he returns in autumn he doesn't have to walk as seriously and disturb the area when it's time to hunt. He noted that scouting an area always causes disturbance and it could take several days to settle down—by doing this in the spring, the ambush site is fresh and ready to hunt in autumn.

If you have read this book in its entirety, you probably found that many tactics sounded similar to those provided by the individuals of this chapter. Yet several methods had a different approach, which I hope you take to heart. Like me, these hunters have been through the school of hard knocks. Sometimes, it takes a few beatings to find what works and what doesn't. This book should help, but in truth, nothing beats hands-on experience when it comes to ambushing a trophy buck, because an educated whitetail will teach you far more than an educated hunter.

Bibliography

2003 Readership Study
   F+W Publications, 2003, *Deer & Deer Hunting Magazine*

Bowhunting Records of North American Whitetail Deer, Second Edition
   Pope and Young Club, 2003

Miller, Karl V., and R. Larry Marchinton. *Quality Whitetails: The Why and How of Quality Deer Management*. Stackpole Books, 1995.

Ozoga, J. J., and L. J. Verme. "Activity Patterns of White-Tailed Deer During Estrus"
   Journal of Wildlife Management Vol. 39, No. 4 (1975): 679–83.

Records Database, www.booneandcrockettclub.com
   Boone and Crockett Club, 2005

The Wildlife Management Institute. *White-tailed Deer, Ecology and Management*
   Stackpole Books, 1984.

Index

About the Author

Born in 1946, award-winning journalist John Trout, Jr. began hunting with both firearm and bow in the 1960s, and has hunted throughout much of North America, including Canada and Mexico. His writing has appeared in magazines including *Field & Stream, Outdoor Life, Petersen's Hunting, Petersen's Bowhunting,* and *Bowhunter,* and he has written numerous books on hunting: *Trailing Whitetails, Hunting Farmland Bucks, Nuisance Animals, The Complete Book of Wild Turkey Hunting, Solving Coyote Problems, Finding Wounded Deer,* and *Hunting Rutting Bucks.*

A father of four, with ten grandchildren, Trout began his outdoor writing and photography career in 1985, inspired in large part by his wife Vikki, also an avid hunter. He observes that it is his time in the woods and passion for the outdoors that led him to pursue trophy whitetails, and has taken several Pope-and-Young-caliber bucks. Trout also believes that challenging hunts have helped him to become a better writer and photographer.

Trout resides in Fairfield, Illinois.